COUNTRYSTYLE
gardens

COUNTRY STYLE
gardens

EDITED BY VICTORIA CAREY
OF COUNTRY STYLE MAGAZINE

HarperCollins*Publishers*

contents

I love tracking down great stories to fill the pages of *Country Style*. We've covered everything from the former Governor-General Quentin Bryce's country childhood to historic properties in Tasmania, but one of the most challenging assignments was finding a peony garden to photograph. I would locate a magnificent peony farm in Tasmania and be told to "visit in November", only to discover, when the time came, that those elusive flowers had already come and gone, with just a few stragglers left.

Finally, after a few years on the peony hunt, I managed to unearth some beautiful stories and one of my favourites is on the cover of this book — Spring Hill Peony Farm in central Victoria. Ironically, owner Mac Barry didn't know what a peony was when he bought the farm — it was all his grandmother's idea. "I asked what grew well around here … and she said, 'Look at peonies,'" Mac recalls. "I'd never heard of them!" I was delighted he took her advice — and you can see the 'peony paddock' in this book.

"I've inherited his love of flowers and I like nothing more than visiting a beautiful garden."

Many of you may have started your gardening days helping a grandparent tend their garden — I know I did. I still remember the wonderful scent of my poppa's tea roses in summer and the dense hedges of camellias with their glossy green leaves. I've inherited his love of flowers and I like nothing more than visiting a beautiful garden. A memorable one was Don Schofield's Blue Mountains property, Winterwood. Much like my grandfather, Don spends all day in his magnificent garden, which is filled with rare plants.

I'm still learning how to garden and I think I always will be. Working on this book, looking at the many wonderful gardens our photographers and writers have visited over the years, has inspired me again — I hope these pages have the same effect on you.

Victoria

in the pink

NO MATTER THE SHADE OR VARIETY, BLUSH
TONES MAKE A DELIGHTFUL STATEMENT, BE IT
A FIELD OF PEONIES OR A CASCADE OF ROSES.

ROSY OUTLOOK

CARVED OUT OF MUDDY PADDOCKS,
THIS VICTORIAN GARDEN NOW
PROUDLY DISPLAYS 450 ROSE VARIETIES.

The 'Seduction' rose is a soft contrast to the vibrant colours of lavender and the rose 'Lavender Dream' opposite.

CLOCKWISE, FROM TOP LEFT 'Henri Matisse', a modern French rose; the mudbrick house; 'Jude the Obscure' is a David Austin variety; beyond the box hedging is a bed filled entirely with red roses. FACING PAGE 'Lavender Dream' is a prolific shrub rose.

The garden's careful plan is in contrast to the informal eucalypts and the massed flowers, while the fountain layout helps direct the eye.

'Buff Beauty' and 'General
Gallieni' compete with
clematis for space in the sun.
FACING PAGE 'Gertrude
Jekyll' is a very fragrant
David Austin variety.

Behind the purple flowers of *Verbena bonariensis* is 'Pierre de Ronsard', with 'Lamarque' climbing over the arbour on the right.

Gold-standard garden design is almost always an exercise in subtle understatement. A casual visitor may be barely aware that a landscape has been subtly altered, particularly in the season when beds are overflowing with masses of roses and colourful perennials.

Such is the case at Paulette and Warwick Bisley's garden, at Coldstream in Victoria's Yarra Valley. "I love a tapestry of flowers," Paulette says. "I confess I'm something of a voyeur of all gardens — although I don't like hot, dry and dusty!" In late summer at the Bisleys', most of the 450 rose varieties seem to be staging a full-scale riot, while dense canopies of deciduous leaves cast welcome shade. The smooth lawns contrast with thick ribbons of evergreen hedges, and colourful perennials fill every available corner.

But it was not always so. Starting with muddy cow paddocks, the initial design concept was developed by landscaper Robert Boyle in 1997, working with architect John Pizzey, who designed the mudbrick house. "The best advice we had from Robert was to enlarge our dam to give us a two-year water capacity," Paulette says. "We would have lost the garden had we not."

The aim was to preserve the views of the Yarra Valley and its many vineyards, and yet provide windbreaks. As Paulette explains, "We're exposed to both north and south. And as well as the winds, the eucalypts are a challenge, as they take so much moisture from the surrounding beds."

The first phase of Robert's plan was completed in early 1999. This included the large formal garden with its fountain and beautiful pergolas. Later phases have included gardens and lawns around the house, plus a large vegetable plot. In 2008, some lawn was eliminated to make way for a new birch grove leading to a crabapple walk.

Robert's careful orchestration of the one-hectare space is evident in the green expanses of grass, backed by the solid mass of an escallonia hedge and by carefully pruned mounds of box. Steps and gravel paths lead the visitor from one corner to another.

The structural skeleton of the garden is only truly apparent when the more ephemeral flowering plants are cut back in winter. Chief among these beauties are Paulette's hundreds of roses. "I really love all roses — but they must have perfume," she says firmly. It's an eclectic mix, ranging from modern hybrid teas and David Austin English roses to Australian-bred climbers and petite floribundas. Roses drape the pergolas, line driveways, decorate walls and fill the air with fragrance.

In the expansive formal centrepiece with a fountain at its heart, four massive beds are packed with roses and informal groups of perennials, carefully selected for colour harmony.

"In each bed I've tried to select tall growing roses and then fill with smaller plantings around them," Paulette says. "Just two roses I grow have little perfume — 'Pierre de Ronsard' and 'Elina' — but their good looks overcome my prejudice against their light perfume."

Paulette's favourites are many. They range from the simplicity of *Rosa rugosa* 'Alba' to the shrub rose 'Sally Holmes', and from the 1899 French tea rose 'General Gallieni' to a modern Gallic offering, 'Henri Matisse', and the unusual scarlet *Rosa moyesii* 'Geranium'.

Paulette's next most treasured plant is salvia. "The many varieties of salvia are the saving grace of most Australian gardens," she declares. "I particularly love *Salvia leucantha* 'Santa Barbara', which holds the garden together until winter. It's very showy in colour — a bit like a Hollywood barmaid!" Borders of lavender and erigeron are used to link beds.

"Over the years the garden has evolved to meet the idiosyncrasies of the site and climate," Paulette says. "After the latest drought, the hardy, dry-tolerant plants that had survived then succumbed in the wet; the bush rats and rabbits do a lot of damage. But then the roses just sulked in the wet years — and come those merciless summer days, they smile; sunburnt but happy!"

border crossing

INSPIRED BY VISITS TO BEAUTIFUL PROPERTIES, A VICTORIAN
COUPLE'S GARDEN SPILLS INTO THE PADDOCK NEXT DOOR.

Box-edged beds filled with
perennials, grasses and roses
enliven the rear of this house
in Newlyn, near Ballarat.

A 'Frühlingsgold' rose sprawls over a statue. FACING PAGE, CLOCKWISE, FROM TOP LEFT 'Mary Queen of Scots' rose; hornbeam (*Carpinus betulus*) with catmint (*Nepeta* 'Six Hills Giant'); *Viburnum sargentii* 'Onondaga'; 'Chanticleer' pears with dwarf periwinkle.

Poppies and roses add colour to the thriving kitchen garden, which expands into the neighbour's paddock.

CLOCKWISE, FROM TOP LEFT Box hedges define the beds; 'Paul's Scarlet' hawthorn is part of a mixed hedge; 'Rose de Rescht' (left) and 'La Reine Victoria' roses climb tripods in the kitchen garden; *Rosa chinensis* 'Mutabilis'. FACING PAGE A golden elm and 'Frühlingsgold' roses light up the parterre.

FACING PAGE
These mounds of *Rosa spinosissima* attract wrens and finches.

Gardeners often start with modest ambitions only to find they've embarked on a grand design. This is what happened to Andrew Lowth and Nigel Smith when they bought a house on a hectare of land in Newlyn, 25 kilometres north-east of Ballarat, in 2005. "There was a boundary between the old garden and the sheep paddock and we thought we'd just plant a few trees in the paddock — we didn't want the garden to be too big," Nigel says.

Famous last words, as the paddock now contains much more than a few trees. Yet it's easy to see how the project grew and grew, for the yearning to create a beautiful country garden was what drew the pair from city life in Sydney to this region of central Victoria, famed for its highly productive volcanic soil and cool highland climate.

Their property also evolved as they took inspiration from Dutch garden designer Piet Oudolf, and from visits to such famous English gardens as Hidcote, Great Dixter and Rousham. Ironically, the most pervasive influence came from almost next door, with a visit to Musk Farm, the home and garden of late interior designer Stuart Rattle.

"Musk Farm in Daylesford was the garden that most inspired us," Andrew says. "There was a sense of magic. You'd walk in the gates and didn't know where to go first — the mystery made you want to explore. It was about design and plants and beauty, and was the best we had seen in Australia. We came home with a lot of ideas."

He and Nigel started in the backyard, which sloped uphill away from the house and featured a concrete path, a clothes hoist and some chicken sheds. "The land sloped so much the house was nearly underground at the back," Nigel recalls. "We made the first garden room there."

They excavated soil from the back of the house and built a drystone retaining wall. On the upper level, they mapped out six beds, edged with gravel paths and neatly clipped box, and filled them with favourite perennials, grasses and roses that are colour-graded. "There are hot colours in the middle bed and then there are the purples and reds, which was inspired by Hidcote," Nigel points out. "That's where we put dark tulips, *Allium giganteum*, ornamental rhubarb and crimson roses like 'Munstead Wood', 'Henri Martin' and 'Scabrosa'."

In a corner, a magnificent pale yellow 'Frühlingsgold' rose arches over an unusual statue, which they found in an antiques shop, and a tall deciduous hedge of hornbeam (*Carpinus betulus*) makes a dense wall enclosing the space. "This garden is changing constantly, as our tastes have changed," Nigel says. "These borders were in more of a prairie style but we've softened them over time."

Andrew and Nigel, who work in the public health system, bring different expertise to the garden. Andrew is the plantsman and Nigel the designer. "Nigel likes structure and architecture, and I love plants and 'Fill it up!'" says Andrew. "It's a good combination in a garden team."

Their "first incursion into the paddock" from the old garden was the establishment of a pear walk, with the white flowering *Pyrus calleryana* 'Chanticleer' underplanted with white dwarf periwinkle (*Vinca minor*) and enclosed in dark green walls of tough, fast-growing privet. "In spring it's all green and white," Nigel says.

The next 'room' was planted with a beech woodland of three or four varieties and four golden oaks (*Quercus robur* 'Concordia') in a grassy meadow. "In 10 years time they'll shade out all the grass and we'll underplant with bluebells," Andrew says. Next to it, a hedged orchard that has proved too shady is still a work in progress. "One of the things I've learnt is that it's best not to make a decision in a hurry," he adds. "You might have 10 ideas and one might be the right one."

The kitchen garden brings year-round pleasure and productivity. "We're out here all the time," says Andrew, running his eye down the rows of raspberries and gooseberries, and neat beds bristling with artichokes, asparagus, leeks, snow peas, broad beans, King Edward potatoes and strawberries. And more roses, some climbing rustic tripods. "Here's 'Rose de Rescht', 'La Reine Victoria' and *Rosa chinensis* 'Mutabilis'," he says. "I pick them all and love having flowers in the house."

Andrew and Nigel see their garden as a compilation of ideas from some of the world's most beautiful spaces, interpreted in an expression of their own creativity. The shady woodland and entry at the side of the house is the place Andrew loves most, because it's filled with many of his favourites — cyclamens, meadowsweet (*Filipendula ulmaria*) and the little dusky cranesbill (*Geranium phaeum*) among them. "There's beautiful stuff in there," he says.

Nigel simply savours the overall experience of being in the garden. "And it doesn't matter what your day has been like," he says. "It's the time after being in the garden that makes it seem like everything's fine in the world."

EVERLASTING LOVE

NURTURED BY ITS OWNER'S LIFELONG PASSION
FOR ROSES, THIS RESPLENDENT OASIS OFFERS
AN INTOXICATING REWARD FOR THE SENSES.

'Chartreuse de Parme' is a Delbard rose. FACING PAGE Snapdragons beside the fragrant 'Jubilee Celebration'.

Wisteria with ivy geraniums on either side. FACING PAGE Pink 'Simply Magic' roses, bearded irises, poppies and purple-leaved plum trees flourish.

CLOCKWISE FROM TOP LEFT Bob Melville and his partner, Tess Lauder; David Austin's 'Gertrude Jekyll'; looking towards the crabapple walk covered in David Austin's 'Ambridge Rose'; a glorious peony poppy. FACING PAGE A bronze gleditsia tree.

In the centre of the
Japanese box hedging
is a bay tree, while
a red 'Satchmo' rose
blooms on the right.

BLUSHING PINK ICEBERG

A few poppies flower amid 'Blushing Pink Iceberg' — "one of the newer roses", according to Bob. FACING PAGE Peony poppies make a splendid showing.

Ask rose expert Bob Melville which bloom he prefers best and he's a little nonplussed. "Well, that's like asking who your favourite friend is," he says, looking around at the hundreds of flowers on his Carmel property in the Perth Hills. "'Pat Austin' is a fantastic rose," he says, gesturing to a stand of apricot-coloured roses. "That will flower all winter if you allow it and it's got beautiful foliage. Over there's 'Chartreuse de Parme', a Delbard rose, that's a real purple with a beautiful fragrance … and then there's 'Double Delight', that's a very fragrant rose, too."

Bob has had time to cultivate a few favourites: he has been growing roses for more than 50 years. He tended his first plants as a 10-year-old, working at his father's orchard and nursery. In 1977 he began his own nursery with four hectares and $100.

Bob quickly built up a reputation for his varied collection. "It was well known that if you wanted a rose you couldn't find anywhere else, you'd go to Melville Nurseries. But the rose industry back then was tough and there wasn't a great deal of money."

Difficult times called for inventive thinking, so Bob changed the way roses were grown and sold. "We moved away from bare-rooted roses and started selling them in pots," he says. "This was one of the first places in the world to grow roses commercially for retail in pots."

Streams of visitors arrive every day to buy roses, wander about the four-hectare gardens and enjoy the view from the café. A willow-wreathed lake near the entrance is picturesque, but has a practical function, too: it's a back-up water supply for the nursery roses growing in the southern half of the property. The middle of the estate is a rambling warren. Arbours of hardy crabapple trees form dappled walkways; their purple-pink foliage interrupted with shocks of climbing 'Crepuscule' and creamy 'Ambridge Rose'. At the heart of the property, an oval-shaped lawn is an orderly counterpoint to the myrtle luma-edged garden beds jumbled with twists of peony poppies, valerian and bearded irises.

Bob pauses at a group of tumbling roses, each with a picket stake at its base painted with its varietal name. He planted this section back in 1986 when he was awarded the agency to sell David Austin roses in Western Australia. These plants are a particular passion for him. "I do like the David Austins best," Bob says. "They're

spectacular and they often flower for nine months of the year. I chased the agency for years."

A steep driveway leads to the home that Bob shares with his partner, Tess Lauder, and to his traditional, French-style garden. It's a marked departure from the free-flowing grounds below. "It's nice and structured, and to me, that's more romantic," Bob says. "And there's lots of green turf to play on and have parties!"

In this section, hedges of Japanese box form calligraphic curves around bay trees and ornamental cabbages (which Bob admits he's not good at growing).

What he is good at growing, not surprisingly, is roses. "The most important thing to remember when growing roses is sunlight, and to plant them in a nice, open mix of soil with a lot of organic material, and some sand," he says.

"The biggest mistake I see is that when spring comes, people haven't mulched. They see the roses start to droop and put a bit of water on them, but it's too late: the plant has already used all of its reserves. You've got to maintain the water. Twice a week is sufficient but don't allow the soil to dry out and then try to get the moisture back in.

"And I don't really like drippers," he adds. "Mother Nature waters from above and the plants love it; they like to be cleansed at least once a week."

The widespread perception that roses require a lot of watering has been bad for business. "We've probably lost half of our production because of the push to grow natives and not use water," Bob says. "But roses are drought-tolerant after 12 months, so if you don't water them, they won't die — they won't look that good, but they won't die on you."

He has his own views on the evolution of rose growing. "Everyone likes to say that the old roses have more fragrance, but I think they're getting more fragrance now than they've ever had. And we're also seeing more disease-resistant roses and more colour. People are demanding a lot more from their roses — they've got to be foolproof now."

Bob says he hasn't lost his love for roses, despite the hard work involved. "I'm working more than 90 hours a week, but it's still a passion," he says. "And this is a beautiful place for growing roses — probably one of the best places in the world."

bloom time

HOW AN ARCHITECT AND A FINANCIAL
TRADER FOUND LOVE AND RAISED A FAMILY
ON A CENTRAL VICTORIAN PEONY FARM.

Co-owner Mac Barry started flower farming to finance his racehorses. FACING PAGE Showing the way to the public pickers who visit the farm.

A mix of 'Felix Supreme' and 'Felix Crousse'. The flowering season lasts only four to six weeks. FACING PAGE Some 10,000 peonies have been planted so far.

The peony has been revered throughout history and many consider it one of the world's most beautiful blooms. Mac Barry and Nicky Thomas may well be the flower's greatest fans, each spring eagerly awaiting the first buds on their farm in central Victoria. But there was a time when neither knew a peony from a pansy.

In 2000, when Mac was still single and bought land at Spring Hill, he wanted to plant a crop that would be profitable enough to fund his hobby of racehorse breeding. Wisely, he sought advice from his grandmother, who lived in the region. "I asked what grew well around here and she said 'Bulbs,' because of the frost," Mac says. "I thought one daffodil stem doesn't sell for much, so she said, 'Look at peonies' … and I'd never heard of them!"

Today, Mac and Nicky, who married in 2006, live and breathe peonies during the flowering burst in November. With their eight-year-old twins, William and Lucinda, they live on a 28-hectare farm in the rich, rolling volcanic country between Daylesford and Kyneton. The highest paddock, two hectares ringed by giant old eucalypts, is planted with peonies — 10,000 of them, to be precise. Cattle graze on the rest of the property, along with Mac's other love, half a dozen thoroughbreds bred for the track.

For much of the year, peonies are undemanding, which allows Nicky and Mac to concentrate on their professions. Nicky is an architect — "For half the year I do mostly domestic renovating" — in between juggling the twins' school and other activities. Mac is a global equities trader for an overseas company, working part of the week in his home office and flying to Sydney for the remainder. But come mid-November, the pace quickens when the first peony buds appear. And then it's all hands on deck.

For two weeks, they and casual workers frantically pick, sort and package the buds, selling them to florists, markets interstate and at farmers' markets around Melbourne. Then the paddock slowly transforms into rows of white, pale and deep pink blooms, 30 or so stems on each plant.

Once the buds unfurl, Nicky and Mac open the paddock over two weekends for visitors to pick their own. "We have too many flowers and it was a way of not wasting them," Nicky says. "Even then we're flat out with people who, for $20, can pick an armful."

In 2012, they bought a deconsecrated 1890s church that backs on to their property. With a modern, pavilion-style building beside it, this now functions as an events venue. It's a good tie-in. "We already supply peonies for loads of weddings and now we've got the church, with quite a few bookings already for next spring," Nicky says.

Mac always wanted to be a farmer. His dad was a stock agent and Mac spent time with him on farms and at saleyards, and on his grandparents' farm near Kyneton. He studied agricultural economics and worked overseas, saving for a deposit on some land. When his grandmother suggested growing a plant he knew nothing about, he hit the books and the internet, and quizzed peony growers.

He also canvassed his mother, sister and grandmother for their opinion on colours. "We narrowed it down to white, pink and dark pink," he says. "Dad helped me put a few in … actually 7000, and they went well." Then Mac flew back to his job at a Tokyo investment bank, leaving the property under his father's watchful eye.

He and Nicky met on a flight to Tokyo in 2002. Mac was returning to work, while Nicky was on her way back to her job with an architectural firm in Ireland. She spent her childhood in Victoria's Apollo Bay and in the nearby Otway Ranges on her grandparents' farm. "My grandfather had stockhorses — my dream is to have a stockhorse," she says. With much in common, Nicky and Mac clicked. "We wrote big email letters to each other after that, until I thought I'd better come back and check him out."

Six months after they met, Mac introduced her to Spring Hill. "We went up to the farm and camped and planted more peonies," Nicky says. "It was decided — I'd move to Japan with Mac. It worked and we stayed there for another three-and-a-half years."

While in Tokyo, they bought an adjoining four hectares at Spring Hill with a century-old woolshed that had been partly converted to a home. They returned for good in 2006 and started renovating. "There were lean-tos on the side so we stripped those off and fixed it up," Nicky says. "Then we extended, as we intended to have children."

Life at Spring Hill affords the right balance between country and city, work and family and recreation. There are plans for a pony for William and Lucinda. As for the peonies, they'll soon be adding a red variety to the mix.

"We put them in the house, a mix of colours and textures, and I adore them all," Nicky says. "The season is short, but we've found that so many people love peonies, too … We didn't know that before!"

Beds edged in brick and stone are full of valerian, irises and agapanthus. FACING PAGE 'Cécile Brünner' is one of 75 rose bushes in the garden.

all in the family

A MOVE TO THE COUNTRY
HAS BROUGHT THREE
GENERATIONS TOGETHER
AROUND A LOVELY GARDEN.

CLOCKWISE, FROM
TOP LEFT Plantings of
valerian in pink, white and
purple; Teresa Eather (right)
with her daughter Erica and
mother-in-law, Judy; the
spiky symmetry of a globe
artichoke; the homestead
overlooks quarter horses
beside a dam. FACING
PAGE Judy uses an old
outhouse as a toolshed.

The beautiful view of the Nundle hills was part of the attraction for Teresa and her husband, Mark.

The first time Mark and Teresa Eather visited Wombramurra homestead, near Nundle in the Peel Valley of northern NSW, it was 1996 and they were guests at their friends' wedding. They attended another wedding here 18 years later, but this time around it had been their home for five years.

They used to live in Sydney, where Mark was a financial trader, but he and Teresa spent nearly every school holiday with their children — James, now 18, Emily, 16, and Erica, 11 — on their 1600-hectare farm at Quirindi on the state's north-west slopes. They wanted them to have a full-time country life. "We always preferred the children to enjoy a farm upbringing, to teach them life's basics," Teresa says.

They sold that farm in 2006 and bought Wombramurra and 200 hectares in 2007. "I'd visited here several times to buy bulls," says rural-raised Mark. "It had a reputation and anyone within 100 kilometres knew of it."

Teresa was more used to big-city living. She spent the first nine years of her life in bustling Hong Kong before moving to Sydney with her family. So, for her, forging a life in the country was a brave move.

To ease themselves into their new world, they initially visited Wombramurra with the kids only during school holidays, but moved here permanently in 2010, initially on a two-year trial. "It was a gentle transition," Teresa says. "I had a chance to meet people and it's easier to make friends when you have children."

She now tutors debating at Nundle Public School, is a member of several volunteer committees and has also started a fashion accessories store and online business, Sacs On Jenkins, in Nundle's main street. Meanwhile, Mark continues to trade financial products.

They graze sheep and Hereford cattle on their land, and breed quarter horses. The property also boasts a small timber museum, a re-creation of the original 1840s Wombramurra homestead, which houses memorabilia of the Payne family, who owned it for nearly 100 years. On a wall are certificates dated 1931 from the Tamworth Pastoral & Agricultural Association — first prize for gladioli, and second prize for dahlias, cannas and cosmos.

Since the couple moved to Wombramurra, the property has become a true family affair, with Mark's parents, Phil and Judy, moving into a cottage near the main homestead. Judy loves being chiefly responsible for the upkeep of the beautiful garden, which was established by the Paynes.

When the previous owners, Peter and Judy Howarth, bought it from the Payne family in 1987, the garden was overgrown and they worked hard to restore it, uncovering rows of stone-edged garden beds, some exquisite stone walls and many trellises.

But now Judy Eather has become the loving custodian, and she and Teresa are animated as they discuss their favourite aspects of the garden. These range through Manchurian pears, sculptural pomegranate fruit, mass plantings of primulas, sedums, irises, agapanthus, daffodils, snowdrops, jonquils, day lilies, spider lilies, valerian, poppies and love-in-a-mist, as well as surprises such as an abundance of tulips and the purple garlic pompom seed balls. An ornamental grapevine, with old wood thicker than a man's wrist, grows over a steel and wire frame, and helps to create a wonderful reading room.

"It is a relaxing garden," says Judy as she enjoys homemade orange muffins and coffee with Teresa, Mark and Phil. "The garden can be appreciated from many different angles, and I very much enjoy the colour schemes that emerge throughout the seasons, from yellow and white to pink."

Teresa and Mark have planted avenues of Lombardy poplars and lipstick maples along the fence and the driveway. It is a form of succession planning for when they may lose some of the oaks and golden elms that are more than a century old.

Mark explains that seeing the children develop a close relationship with their grandparents is one of the greatest rewards of their country move. Phil and Erica share time together when they feed a calf every morning. James, Erica and Emily help Phil and Mark feed horses and muster cattle, and everyone assists Judy in the garden. "I've lived on the land all my life, and used to collect flowers and display them in saucers of water," Judy says of her own childhood. "Now Erica does the same thing."

Alongside these happy daily rituals, there were wedding preparations afoot in 2011 when Mark's Sydney-based sister, Jane Eather, married Hayden Elton. Judy wasn't the slightest bit surprised when her daughter readily accepted Mark and Teresa's offer to have the wedding at Wombramurra.

"Jane is a real family girl," Judy says. "There was a high tea in the garden. She had all the nieces and nephews involved. Emily and Erica were flower girls."

RESTORING ORDER

THIS SOUTHERN QUEENSLAND GRAZING PROPERTY UNDERGOES
A WONDERFUL REGENERATION AFTER IT INSPIRED A COUPLE.

Sedum 'Autumn Joy' attracts an even more colourful visitor to the Dalveen garden. FACING PAGE Looking north to the cattle paddocks across the scented garden.

A pin oak towers over ground cover of agave, *Miscanthus sinensis* and Russian sage. FACING PAGE, CLOCKWISE, FROM TOP LEFT

The homestead's turret was added in the early 1900s; a 'Jasmina' weeping standard rose; lavender, rosemary and briar roses; *Rosa* 'Mutabilis'.

A David Austin 'England's Rose'.
FACING PAGE A topiary arch of
star jasmine frames the view of
the arbour behind a pink 'Queen
Elizabeth' and an 'Iceberg' rose.

Phil and Kristen Richards looked for a rural property for a year before luck came their way during a 2009 weekend in the country to celebrate their 25th wedding anniversary. The couple were driving along the New England Highway between Warwick and Stanthorpe in southern Queensland when Kristen spotted the distinctive turret of the Braeside homestead rising above the tree line.

Their interest was immediately caught by the 1874 homestead, high on the bank of Turner Creek near the village of Dalveen. "We fell in love," Kristen recalls. "We thought, 'This is it, this is the one.'"

Based in Brisbane, the Richards are keen gardeners who yearned to find land where they could create a cool-climate garden. "We've always had a garden in Brisbane but with a limited palette," Phil explains.

On the edge of Queensland's Granite Belt and with temperatures dipping as low as minus nine in winter, Braeside certainly had cool credentials. And there was another important factor — the opportunity to rehabilitate run-down agricultural land. The couple are admirers of the Natural Sequence Farming approach to regeneration developed by Australian agricultural pioneer Peter Andrews in the 1970s. The 495 hectares of degraded, rocky country with an overgrown creek presented a great opportunity, and they bought the heritage-listed property just a few months later.

Gardening and pasture restoration began the following year, and Tenterfield garden designer Carolyn Robinson was engaged as a consultant. Her first task was to rescue Turner Creek, which was inaccessible, having been covered with weeds and thick scrub. Excavators created terraced pathways along the bank below the existing garden, and granite boulders were placed in the creek bed to slow water flow and reduce erosion. Then basket grass (*Lomandra longifolia*) was planted along the creek to help secure the bank.

Over the past five years, almost 12 hectares surrounding the homestead have been developed, with parkland plantings to complement existing trees. Gravel mulch is used to improve water efficacy, and the light clay loam is enriched with mushroom compost and lime. "We like to give the trees a good start," Phil says. "But after that, there's no fertilising program. We try to keep things ticking over on their own."

The driveway at the entrance was resurfaced with cobblestones and, close to the homestead, a series of formal garden areas were created, with roses such as 'Queen Elizabeth', 'Gold Bunny' and 'St Patrick' providing structure. A 95-year-old Aleppo pine (*Pinus halepensis*) was grown from seed that, legend has it, was brought back from Gallipoli's Lone Pine battlefield by a local soldier.

Descending to the paved terrace just below the formal homestead garden is an ideal vantage point from which to view the creek walk and the parkland beyond Turner Creek. "We love to have our morning coffee here, or a late afternoon drink when the sun spills across," Phil says.

The Mediterranean-themed garden in this section is a patchwork of silver, shot through with pink and purple, and contains olives, salvia, English and Italian lavender, agastache and purple sage. The perennial beds along the creek walk are lined by hedges of Portuguese laurel and framed by dry-rock walls.

To the east, where a bridge leads to the flood plain, is the parkland, with English and Spanish oaks, claret ashes, chestnuts and golden elms planted among established apple gums, and yellow and grey box. On the northern side, a parterre garden has deciduous trees such as maples, crabapples and snow pears. The overlooking sandstone terrace with a view is where Phil and Kristen enjoy summer breakfasts and twilight dinners. Below is a scented rose garden "designed for wandering" with underplanting of dianthus, butterfly bush and Easter daisies.

With the main structures within the garden almost complete, the surrounding paddocks — where a herd of some 80 Charolais breeding cattle grazes — are part of a longer restoration project. The cutting back of the wattle regrowth and pasture re-seeding are well underway.

There have been challenges, from harsh frosts and drought to rabbits invading the garden. "Plenty of times we thought, 'What on earth are we doing? Have we lost our minds?'" Phil admits. "However, we've had the privilege of creating something alive and beautiful that can endure, and be enjoyed, for generations."

Braeside has become a much-loved retreat for Phil and Kristen, along with their four adult children and two grandchildren. Their daughter was married in the garden in October 2014. "They say to us, 'You can never sell it!'" Kristen says. "There's a special connection here."

Brian Wagner takes flowers to market. FACING PAGE Two Delbard roses, the pink 'Sister Emmanuelle' and striped 'Maurice Utrillo'.

love bloomed

A SOUTH AUSTRALIAN ROSE GROWER FOUND
HIS ITALIAN PARTNER ON A CYCLING ODYSSEY.

'Paul Cezanne', another Delbard rose. FACING PAGE, CLOCKWISE, FROM TOP LEFT 'Sister Emmanuelle' is one of 650 varieties grown on the property; "I see the best sunrises every day," Brian says; 'Valencia' and the multicoloured 'Eyes For You'; son Luca inspects the apricot 'Valencia'.

Benedetta Rusconi, an Italian photojournalist, was in Ireland's Aran Islands working on a travel feature in 2003 when she came across a cyclist towing a trailer filled with golf clubs and camping gear.

"I thought, 'Wow, this is an interesting person!' " she says. "He seemed a very happy man …"

The bloke on the bike was South Australian rose grower Brian Wagner, a man partial to an adventure who had previously pedalled around China and India. As fate would have it, the intrepid traveller checked into the same hostel as Benedetta, and the pair became friends over dinner. A fortnight later, she was showing Brian around her Milan home. "I didn't quite make it all the way around Ireland," says Brian with a smile.

For the next three years, they pursued a long-distance relationship, meeting in destinations dictated by magazine assignments and flower seasons, until Benedetta agreed to pack up her apartment and give Australian life a go. For the first 12 months, she was based in Adelaide, studying commercial photography while Brian worked hard at his rose nursery at Kalangadoo near the Limestone Coast. But the arrival of their son, Luca, now eight, heralded a permanent move to the bush.

"It was such a big change coming from Europe; you find yourself alone in this huge space and it's a strange feeling that's difficult to get used to," Benedetta says. "I would push the pram down the main street of Penola, and stop at every shop and cafe to say hello, and that was a good way to meet people. I would also go to the supermarket and just stare. I still can't believe that you can have a whole row of just potato chips — in Italy we have only two brands!"

Slowly, Benedetta has embraced the gentle rhythm of country life and its freedom of choice, raising Luca and five-year-old daughter Chiara while also pursuing her photography and supporting Brian in the business he had taken over from his parents.

Wagner's Rose Nursery produces around 160,000 rose bushes each season, supplying garden centres nationwide in addition to selling locally at farmers' markets, where buckets of freshly cut blooms are always in high demand. The roses thrive in the fertile paddocks and are some of the best the world has to offer, with the latest releases flown in from gardens around the globe.

"We grow around 650 different varieties of roses, including lots of Delbards and David Austins," Brian says. "The key priorities are plant health and fragrance." A heady scent fills the air at the 50-hectare property, where a line of ancient red gums forms a dramatic backdrop to the rows of exquisite colour. "I see the best sunrises every day," Brian says.

Benedetta has also come to adore the landscape. "I don't like the flies, and there's no escaping the sun and the heat, but Australia gives you such a sense of freedom, and the space is unbelievable," she says. "Your eyes are a wide-angle lens with such a large horizon. This doesn't happen in Europe."

Each year, Benedetta and Brian take the children to a family beach house near the Italian Riviera's Cinque Terre region, and it's Brian who needs to acclimatise.

"I've spent my life surfing remote beaches, so it's taken some time to get used to hiring your own plot of sand, due to the crowds there," he says. "But now I look forward to the routine of buying fresh focaccia for breakfast, going for long walks and just feeling part of a busy village."

While Benedetta savours the familiar smells of the bakery, the fish shop and the patisseries — "You walk with your nose in Italy, but you don't do that here," she says with a smile — Brian tries hard to resist buying every vase he sees.

"He's always looking for vases when he travels and imagining which rose would look best in them," Benedetta explains. "You could go nuts with all that Venetian glass," says Brian with another ready smile.

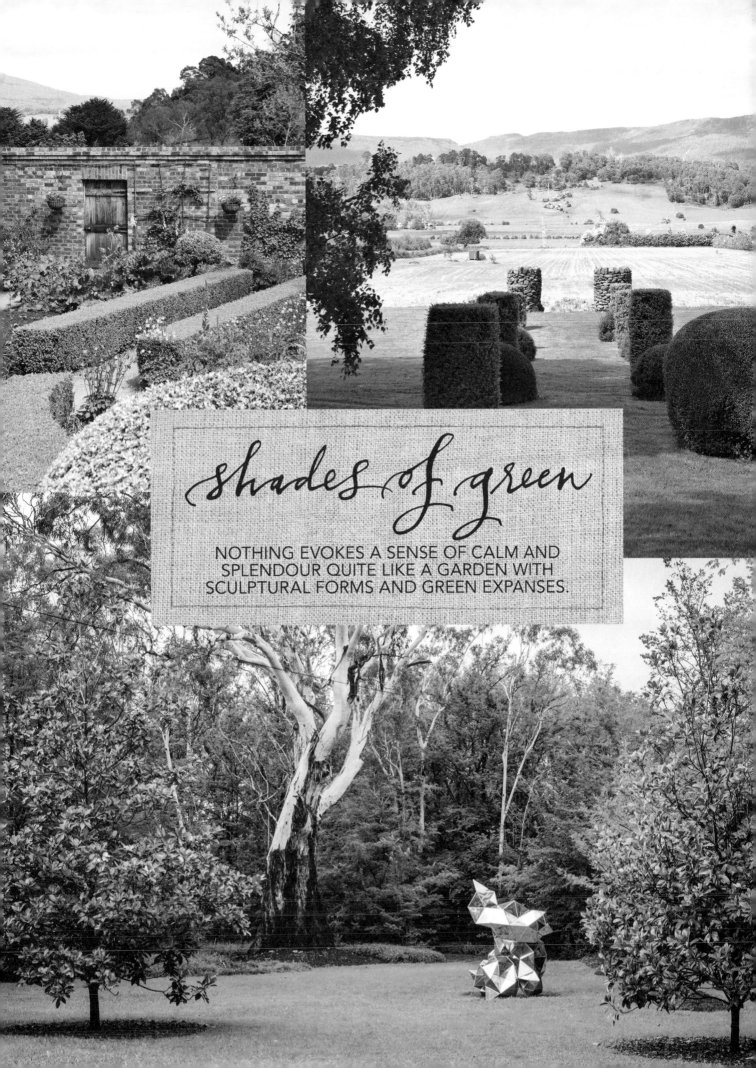

shades of green

NOTHING EVOKES A SENSE OF CALM AND
SPLENDOUR QUITE LIKE A GARDEN WITH
SCULPTURAL FORMS AND GREEN EXPANSES.

FANTASY FOREST

OLD TREES TAKE ON AN IMPRESSIVE NEW LIFE AS
TOPIARY IN THIS GARDEN IN CENTRAL VICTORIA.

The cypresses that kept
coming back have been
sculpted into a stunning
geometric array at
Rosebery Hill near Kyneton.

Ceanothus in bloom.
FACING PAGE A carpet
of bluebells provides a lush
underplanting for the oaks.

This corkscrew topiary has been refined over decades. FACING PAGE, CLOCKWISE, FROM TOP LEFT Owners Ruth and Barry Murphy stroll down the poplar avenue; quince blossom; dark green shapes contrast with the oak leaves above; bladder campion (*Silene vulgaris*), a hardy perennial.

Lilac in bloom. FACING
PAGE The landscape
around the property in
Victoria's Macedon Ranges.

Moving a driveway can effect more changes in a country garden than the route to the front door. Such was the case at Barry and Ruth Murphy's property, Rosebery Hill, where the change led to an outbreak of topiary that has turned part of the extensive garden into a fantasy land.

The story started when the Murphys decided to remove a short drive from the nearby road and create a winding, enticing path through an avenue of trees to their secluded house at Pipers Creek, near Kyneton in central Victoria. Along the old driveway were a few remnant Monterey cypress (*Cupressus macrocarpa*).

"They were about 60 to 70 years old and were falling apart, dropping branches in the wind," Barry recalls. "So we decided to get rid of them."

Ruth adds, "We burnt out the old hearts of each one, but afterwards seedlings kept coming up from the roots. Our idea was to keep them trimmed to eye level, so we didn't have to use a ladder … well, that was the grand idea. But they escaped!"

Thirty years on, Barry has had to get bigger ladders, saying, "I started with a 10-foot one but then had to go to 14-foot!" His designs are improvised — "I didn't start with a plan, I just started trimming" — although the couple do draw inspiration from books and magazines. Today the cypress offspring would be at home in Alice's Wonderland and the quirky, clipped shapes could compete with the astonishing, centuries-old collection of yew topiary at the renowned Levens Hall in England's north.

Barry and Ruth describe their topiary follies, tucked away among mature trees and shrubs, and their entire garden as a triumph of Mother Nature over human endeavour. This is not strictly accurate. A great deal of hard work has gone into fashioning the four-hectare garden and parkland, the cultivated heart of their sheep and cattle property of 108 hectares. Their timber house was built by Ruth's great-grandfather and the property name comes from Rosebery Topping in Yorkshire, where the family lived before migrating to Australia in 1851.

"We love both roses and berries, but the name is really all to do with family connections," Ruth says.

The present driveway, 300 metres long, was carved through the paddocks and bordered with 70 red oaks (*Quercus rubra*) that Barry germinated from acorns. In autumn the trees turn glorious shades of crimson, and in spring the ground beneath the oaks' fresh green leaves is a bluebell-and-daffodil showcase. Indeed, bulbs and roses are highlights, along with flowering shrubs. "Anything with a perfume," says Ruth. But it's the extensive tree collection that's the abiding memory.

Trees are Barry's passion. He has a great interest in conifers and has collected many unusual species. "I love cedars, particularly the Atlas cedar (*Cedrus atlantica*). It's a wonderful tree with a spectacular branching habit. But there are always disappointments … we find that many of the conifers die here after 20 or 30 years. Although we have deep soil, the trees we've planted have to survive without being watered. We live in a true Mediterranean climate. One tree we'll never plant again is the Lawson cypress (*Chamaecyparis lawsoniana*), which we put in early. It needs an annual rainfall of more than 1000 millimetres."

By contrast, oaks, another tree with a strong place in Barry's heart, thrive in this area. He has planted an entire arboretum of nearly 70 species, and that doesn't include a beautiful avenue of cork oaks (*Quercus suber*) leading out to the sheep paddocks. One of his favourites is the Macedon oak (*Quercus trojana*), a hybrid that Barry points out is quite distinctive, with its red leaves holding on into July. A century-old cork oak also commands attention.

An avenue of poplars, five different catalpas, various limes — including the common lime (*Tilia* x *europaea*) with its fragrant flowers — delicate weeping maples and flowering cherries are some of the many other beautiful and unusual trees on the property.

The climate at Pipers Creek is testing for gardeners. "We get severe frosts — minus four degrees — that do a lot of damage, and in summer the hot north winds are terrible," Ruth says. "Our worst day was Black Saturday in February 2010 — the bark on trees was cooked and the sap boiled. Wind, no matter the direction, is the enemy."

They are trying not to expand the garden. "We have a lot of weeding but our biggest job has been removing branches, mostly the lower limbs of the trees that are half dead," Barry says. "Of course, we're removing our mistakes as well! It's heavy work. The aim, especially in winter, is to try and get things under control."

Ruth adds, "We like to start the day with a wander and often get lost in the garden. We come from farmers on both sides of the family … we just need to grow plants and enjoy every new pair of leaves."

amazing grace

WITH MORE THAN 5000
AZALEAS, THIS GARDEN
PROVES THAT 'EXOTIC' PLANTS
CAN BE DROUGHT HARDY —
IT'S ALL IN THE PREPARATION.

Dietes iridioides, a popular perennial also known as wild iris. FACING PAGE Looking out from the garden towards the tree nursery.

CLOCKWISE, FROM TOP LEFT White *Agapanthus africanus*; a Buddha statue nestled among *Azalea* 'Gumpo'; organic vegetables; the courtyard, with Japanese maples (*Acer palmatum* 'Trompenburg'). FACING PAGE Layers of hedging define the garden spaces.

James and Barbara McGeoch's eldest daughter, Kirsty, drew inspiration from her travels to suggest the Tibetan word 'emaho' as a name for their family home in the ranges of Ravensbourne, 135 kilometres north-west of Brisbane. Emaho means 'wonderful' or 'amazing' and it's an apt choice for this tree farm and country garden lying in a crook of the picturesque mountains.

"It fits well here, that's how we feel about the property," Barbara says. Prior to making their home at Emaho, James and Barbara ran a nursery in Brisbane and had also expanded into the international landscaping market. Then they visited some people who lived in Ravensbourne and became enthralled by the towering eucalypt forest and tranquillity of the region. When these friends called in 2000 to say that the 16-hectare property next door was for sale, the McGeochs were quick to seize the opportunity and signed the contract within two weeks.

The rich volcanic soil was one attraction. "We bought it because we liked it, but then we looked at how we could use it as well," Barbara says. "It's perfect for what we do, as it has good drainage."

The McGeochs grow trees at Emaho for domestic and commercial landscape projects: at 600 metres, the farm's elevation provides a sufficiently cool climate to acclimatise the trees destined for southern markets in Australia. However, the couple's main business focus is overseas through Birkdale International, which works on high-profile landscape projects in mainland China, Hong Kong, Macau and Abu Dhabi.

Although the couple could see the property's potential, it was hardly perfect. "It was a cow paddock, covered in stumps and lantana, with falling-down fences," Barbara says bluntly. "We had to clean it up, retain the good trees — and then start planting."

Their first consideration was to secure a reliable irrigation system. They built a dam and put in lines to funnel water so that all rainfall would be captured. Wildlife corridors were created to link with the rainforest below the dam and perimeter planting was set up to shelter the garden.

In 2005, with the building of the cottage complete, the McGeochs began work on the garden. Barbara describes it as "reminiscent of the traditional Australian country garden but with an Asian influence".

The garden soon looked as though it had been established for ages, due to careful preparation and the use of semi-mature trees and mass plantings. Set into the side of a hill, it provides sweeping views of the tree farm and surrounding ranges.

The cottage was positioned to take advantage of passive solar gain, and a courtyard, which sits to the north, features Japanese maples bordered by a *Camellia sinensis* hedge, a copse of Mongolian pear, and golden and claret ashes. "I brought in some trees that were already 10 to 12 years old," Barbara says. "When you get the bones of the garden right, then you can plant a lot of smaller plants underneath."

A path meanders through a forest of crabapples, which gives a stunning display of pink blossom in spring, then winds through massed azaleas, camellias, irises, lavender, Indian hawthorn and agapanthus. The driveway is lined with bamboo (*Bambusa textilis* 'Gracilis'), whose attractive form has the added bonus of acting as an effective wind and dust barrier. Barbara says that preparation is crucial to maximise survival during drought.

"Before planting we soaked the azalea roots in a mixture of seaweed and fish emulsion so that the whole root ball was totally saturated; then we planted and watered them in with that same mix," she explains. "I've got huge swathes of azaleas that have never been watered since they were planted. People often over-water plants, so they tend to develop surface roots — and then when we get a dry spell, the plants suffer."

Barbara has planted 5500 azaleas throughout the property and considers many exotics to be as hardy as natives. "We've created a sustainable garden with plants our clients perceived as not being drought tolerant. We were left with the azaleas when we were closing down the Brisbane nursery — people thought they should be planting natives, but there are many exotic plants that are just as hardy. I really do believe that if you prepare your garden well to start with, you will get a good result."

James and Barbara presented Emaho in the Open Garden Scheme in 2007 — just two years after it was established — and demonstrated what can be achieved by using available resources in an environmentally sustainable system. "It has such a sense of serenity," Barbara says. "It gives me a great sense of satisfaction to see family and friends enjoy it."

SHAPING THE PAST

A RETURN TO AGE-OLD TECHNIQUES, INCLUDING ELEPHANT
TOPIARY, HAS REVITALISED A HISTORIC TASMANIAN ESTATE.

Topiary and stone pillars direct the eye to the Great Western Tiers. FACING PAGE, CLOCKWISE, FROM TOP LEFT An excelsior hybrid foxglove; owners Deb and Scott Wilson; a bumblebee investigates a columbine; clipped shrubs and hedges, fruit trees and flowering plants feature.

The elephant hedge is Old Wesleydale's best-known feature.

A row of silver birches forms the backdrop to plantings of 'Wedding Day' iris and 'Walker's Low' catmint in the black and white garden.

Scott Wilson is having trouble keeping the elephants under control. "The elephant babies have now had babies of their own!" announces his wife, Deb, on our arrival at Old Wesleydale. Old Wesleydale's pachyderms may be running rampant, but they aren't actually real. Instead, they're part of an astonishing topiary hedge that Scott started clipping soon after the family moved to the property, near Mole Creek in northern Tasmania, in 2001.

Inspired by a sculptured hedge they had seen in an English magazine, Scott took the shears to a low hedge of honeysuckle at the front of the two-storey Georgian house. A decade later, keeping the shapes neat and lifelike is a challenge, but Scott's solution is to sculpt a new baby elephant in places where the hedge starts to bulge. "And so the hedge grows and changes every year," Deb explains.

This leafy, now somewhat portly elephant conga line is one of Old Wesleydale's best-known features. For visitors, it's the first inkling that topiary, and other traditional horticultural and landscape crafts, have played a key role in the resurrection of this historic property and its beautiful garden.

Old Wesleydale sits well back from the road to Mole Creek, with views to the dramatic escarpment of the Great Western Tiers across the valley. The grandeur of this 'borrowed landscape', the valley's fertile soils, a 112-centimetre average annual rainfall and the private two-hectare lake were great attractions when the Wilsons came to Tasmania in 1998 to look for a property. At the time they lived in Coolah in NSW's central west, and longed to grow some plants they loved — especially hydrangea and viburnum — with ease.

When the couple finally moved in three years later with their teenage daughters, Kaitlyn and Sally, the hawthorn hedges around the paddocks had been shored up with white wooden rails ("which Scott hated") and there was very little garden planted — just mature trees such as giant liquidambars, silver birches and a weeping elm (*Ulmus* 'Camperdownii') at the front of the house and some eucalypts, acacia and the remnants of an apple orchard at the back. The 97-hectare property also had substantial stone outbuildings, including the original bakehouse in the backyard and a large, walled compound comprising a two-storey barn, stables, smithy and cattle shelters around a central courtyard.

The Wilsons started by building a high brick wall at the rear and laying paths hedged with immaculately clipped tiers of box and *Pittosporum tenuifolium* 'Limelight'. Creating a walled garden that is sheltered from the westerly winds is, according to Scott, "the best thing we've done".

Inspired by the black-and-white garden at Highgrove, the family home of Prince Charles in the UK, Scott and Deb laid out their own version in a paddock at the back of the house. A copse of birch trees is the backdrop to beds of light-flowering, dark-flowering and foliaged perennials, including purple cow parsley (*Anthriscus sylvestris* 'Ravenswing'), Queen Anne's lace (*Daucus carota*), Solomon's seal (*Polygonatum*) and black iris.

Scott and Deb share the gardening, although each has their specialty. "Scott does the hedging — he has a good eye — and I do the planting and most of the weeding," she says.

In 2003, Scott worked on a neighbouring property, Bentley, where he learnt traditional hedge-laying and stonewall building skills under the tutelage of an English artisan commissioned to restore that property's hedges and walls. Old Wesleydale is now benefiting as Scott uses the age-old method of rejuvenating the 170-year-old hawthorn hedges, cutting the trunks almost through and then bending and laying them horizontally one on top of the other. New vertical growth soon weaves through the laid trunks, strengthening, thickening and prolonging the life of the hedge.

Although the Wilsons didn't have a plan for their garden — just a blank canvas and a flexible approach — things have fallen into place almost perfectly. Guests staying in the buttery, which the couple have turned into bed-and-breakfast accommodation, are encouraged to enjoy the garden, whether that's by picking fruit and vegetables for their meals or simply admiring its beauty.

Scott and Deb can now take pleasure watching the maturing garden settle into its historic surrounds as if it had been there forever.

"We've made a garden in each place we've lived, but we've always had to leave it behind before we saw it established," Deb explains. "Our life has changed in so many ways since coming here."

A satisfied Scott agrees, saying, "Yes, we feel like we've died and gone to heaven."

Houdini Cloud, a stainless steel work by Gregor Kregar, stands outside the Upper Hunter Valley gallery, which is flanked by robinias and elms.

OUT OF THE WOODS

A NSW PROPERTY HIDDEN FOR 30 YEARS NOW DISPLAYS
SCULPTURE IN ITS GARDEN BESIDE A THRIVING GALLERY.

CLOCKWISE, FROM TOP LEFT The homestead dates from the 1840s; the original garden plantings included hydrangeas; *Pale Sonata* by artist Lucy Vader hangs by the door; co-owner Michael Reid. FACING PAGE A dog sculpture by Charlotte Drake-Brockman and Fran Wachtel is at home among the robinias and red gums.

FACING PAGE Hydrangeas
and a Cécile Brünner
climbing rose dominate
the side of the house.

Screened by a thicket of self-seeded robinias, alders and golden elm trees, Bobadil, the imposing Georgian house and art gallery belonging to Michael Reid and Nellie Dawes, has a sense of mystery and intrigue — a secret garden.

Travellers on the New England Highway at Murrurundi in NSW's Upper Hunter Valley may catch glimpses of the two-storey house. It was built as a Cobb and Co staging post called the White Swan Inn in the 1840s and then converted to a private home for landholder John Sevil, his wife and 11 children in the early 1900s.

The house and its 4½-hectare garden remain in the Sevil family. For generations it was bequeathed to the eldest unmarried daughter, and its current custodian is John Sevil's great-great-granddaughter, Nellie Dawes.

The immediate past owner, Trixie Kellaher, and Nellie's mother, Leonie Dawes (née Sevil), were cousins. Trixie spent her last 10 years in a nursing home, and the garden was largely untended for three decades.

Buying Bobadil in 2004 renewed Michael and Nellie's connection with the Upper Hunter and Liverpool Plains. Nellie's family is from nearby McDonalds Creek and Michael's grandparents lived in Scone.

The couple's first priority was to remove the almost impenetrable thickets of the noxious weed privet, which encroached on the walls of the house. "Not even people who had lived in the town for a long time had seen the house or garden for 30 years," Michael says.

Over a couple of years, heavy machinery was used to remove 80 truckloads of privet and blackberry bushes, revealing remnants of brick-edged garden beds and the sandstone ruins of a barracks built to house convict road gangs. Michael points out flourishing agapanthus, irises, rosemary, hydrangeas and hibiscus that had lain dormant for decades, which were coaxed to flower once the sun warmed the soil again.

Early in their custodianship, Michael met historian James Broadbent, who encouraged him to adopt a relaxed approach to the project. "James believes that we over-fuss and over-manicure our gardens, while the gardens around many old houses were practical, useful spaces, providing food," Michael says. "The gardens were low-key because the owners didn't have the technology or the desire to over-finesse."

Michael and Nellie, with help from garden designer Kimberly Appleby, divided the garden into useful spaces, creating privacy around the house with towering hedges of cypress and lines of London plane trees. Closer to the gallery is a canopy of robinias, golden elms, alders and eucalypts, underplanted with masses of "what grows" — acanthus, periwinkles, hellebores, irises, hollyhocks, violets and Japanese windflowers.

"The acanthus started with a clump of two plants by the house," Nellie says. "After they've flowered, the dried flowerheads and seeds are mown back into the soil, and they come back the following season."

Gravel crunches underfoot as Michael follows a path meandering past textured tree trunks, his prized golden elm foliage, and the enormous river red gum that anchors the garden.

He and Nellie saw potential in the convict barracks. The remains were dismantled and reassembled, then finished with heavy timber beams reclaimed from a Sydney wool store, a timber apex and doors, and a corrugated iron roof. The resulting gallery became an incubator for emerging artists and a complement to the Michael Reid Art Gallery in Sydney, and later in Berlin.

The garden is an extension of the gallery, and is used for exhibition openings and educational presentations. Michael and Nellie have also opened the Big Brown Dog café — a sheltered corridor between the walls of the sandstone gallery and the robinia forest, it has become Michael's favourite part of the garden.

While Nellie divides her time evenly between Sydney and Murrurundi, Michael travels further afield more often. However, he hopes to spend more time in the garden in future, nurturing a nursery of locally adapted plants, and working with Sydney architect William Zuccon to build a new gallery and renovate Bobadil.

When 'head gardener' Michael is absent, care of the property is the responsibility of Keith Parker and Hayden Kaney. Standing at the entrance, Nellie recalls Keith, who is in his 70s, briefing gardeners from his hospital bed while convalescing after a hip replacement. "Keith is part of the DNA of the house and has a sense of ownership of the garden," Nellie says.

The iron gate squeaks closed and clangs shut on the secret garden — fortunately now a secret to be shared.

into the blue

FROM A CARPET OF BLUEBELLS TO SHOWERS
OF FRAGRANT WISTERIA, FEW COLOURS IN THE
GARDEN DELIGHT LIKE BLUE AND PURPLE.

mountain legacy

THE ORIGINAL VISION
BEHIND A WORLD-FAMOUS
GARDEN IN NSW'S BLUE
MOUNTAINS IS PRESERVED
BY ITS NEW OWNERS.

A 90-year-old *Wisteria floribunda* 'Macrobotrys'. FACING PAGE Nooroo's wisteria draws visitors from around the world.

The property has many century-old trees, including some oaks planted in 1880 that mark the original driveway of the homestead.

A bed of 'Menton' tulips.
FACING PAGE A Japanese
weeping maple, 'Golden
Torch' rhododendron,
'Osaraku' azalea and
Aubrieta 'Axcent Lilac'.

Recalling a British woodland scene, this path wanders through a mass of bluebells and pink miniature pieris.

Wisteria at the rear of the house. FACING PAGE Flanked by forget-me-nots and *Iberis sempervirens*, steps lead to a 'Mollis' azalea and a little summer house.

Nooroo, on Mount Wilson in the Blue Mountains west of Sydney, is world famous for its wisteria collection. But this is far from all it has to offer. From the sensibilities of its early Victorian inhabitants seeking to shape a memory of Europe in a new land, to the bold vision of subsequent owners who brought plants from around the world, many factors have shaped this significant alpine garden. And today Nooroo, though still developing, manages to retain a sense of timelessness: a quality that has captured the imagination of generations of garden lovers and continues to draw visitors from far and wide.

The Valder family are chiefly responsible for Nooroo's legacy. For 75 years, from 1917, they lovingly planted and tended 4.5 hectares of cool-climate trees and shrubs. The magnificent wisteria collection was developed by the eminent botanist Peter Valder. Lorraine and Tony Barrett, two doctors who purchased the property in 1992, owe much to their predecessors, and continue to enjoy a warm relationship with Peter and his brother John.

Nooroo was established in 1880 by William Hay, a Scottish squatter from the Riverina who had become a NSW politician of some note, and who for some years was Mount Wilson's largest landowner. Hay may have been homesick for the green fields of home; in any event, he and other settlers in the area built a southern hemisphere Arcadia, whose orchards and avenues of chestnuts, walnuts and elms created a hillside refuge from the summer heat of Sydney.

Tony says this is what attracted him to the property. "I grew up in Walgett and Collarenebri, in north-west NSW. It's very dry country but we had a strong British influence; our storybooks were filled with meadows of bluebells and that's what we aspired to."

The Barretts have striven not only to maintain the Valder garden but also to stamp their own personality on Nooroo. The first thing to go were the sheep. "There were 29 sheep and I could only ever catch 28 of them," reveals Tony. Then the garden was extended almost by accident when an ancient oak tree "just fell over", creating a new expanse of lawn.

"We were upset about the tree," Tony recalls. "But when I told Peter Valder, he said, 'What can you do? You've got to get over it,' which was evidence of his pragmatic nature." The branches lost exposed shaded beds to new

light; long forgotten plants re-emerged, so too did new opportunities for growth. Accordingly, the Barretts added to the Valder collection with varieties of osmanthus, dogwood, hydrangea, maple, pieris and rhododendron.

One of Tony's favourites is *Rhododendron* 'Fragrantissimum', which competes with the wisteria in the headiness of its aroma. But it is wisteria for which Nooroo is most famed. Peter Valder collected many varieties over the years, from within Australia, and also from Asia, Europe and North America.

"For sheer beauty, the 'Macrobotrys' is my favourite," Tony says. "The flowers are small and ethereal, and the drop of the pendant racemes is more than a metre." A 90-year-old specimen drapes itself over the pergola outside the house, a curtain of purple petals above the gravel drive.

English oaks, chestnuts, ashes and cedars were underplanted with bulbs, including bluebells, daffodils and crocuses. While spring passes in a blur of colour and frenetic activity, Tony laments the hiatus between autumn and winter when the garden can look "sad".

"One of the reasons we planted more was to extend the flowering season," he says. "Wisteria can be fleeting and temperamental. I think rhododendron trees are glorious and, even when the petals fall, the seed pod is very sculptural. And, of course, an old garden like this has the benefit of these magnificent trees."

The trees include oaks, golden ashes, chestnuts, maples, copper beeches, weeping elms, crabapples, lilacs, enkianthus, dogwoods and magnolias. Banks of azalea 'Mollis', beds of peonies, and 'Gertrude Jekyll' and 'Queen Elizabeth' roses form vibrant borders to wild woods that stretch beyond the formal areas.

"Some people come here and they're almost running in circles because they're so excited," Tony says. "The traditionalists hate that the sheep have gone, but some things have to change. Gardens are not static."

Tony takes the job of preserving Nooroo's living history seriously: "None of the plants that were here have been removed; we've pruned but not replaced ... We have occasional help but on the whole we do it ourselves. There would be much more work if it were a newer garden. Some beds have not been weeded in 18 years, as the bulbs are so thickly massed underground. Plus the soil is wonderful here, it's like chocolate!"

room to move

A SERIES OF DEFINED SPACES IS THE HIGHLIGHT OF
THIS GARDEN ON QUEENSLAND'S SOUTHERN DOWNS.

A 1948 pick-up, used as a delivery truck, beneath a jacaranda. FACING PAGE Clematis 'Kiri Te Kanawa'.

Clint Kenny's first impression of Warwick was memorable for all the wrong reasons. "All I remember was cold showers and freezing winter winds," says the landscaper, thinking back to when he travelled to the town 130 kilometres south-west of Brisbane for a polocrosse competition.

Despite his initial misgivings, the self-proclaimed 'rose and rodeo city' quickly grew on him when he returned for a landscape design job. "I loved it straightaway," he says. "I liked the idea of the country lifestyle and it's a great town that's full of history."

Clint made the move in 2003 when he was 22 and later established his garden design business, just two hours drive from clients in Brisbane and close to the Darling Downs and New England regions.

He has gardened for "as long as I can remember" and has fond memories of his grandmother's property in South Australia. "My nanna won the local garden competition so many times they eventually had to make her a judge!" he says.

Clint's hobby led to a job offer while he was working in Brisbane and the career change opened doors to a range of clientele. "I liked it and found I was good at it," he says. "We had great clients in the inner city and did a lot of courtyard installations and balconies."

Yet although his garden design career was blossoming, Clint craved a smaller and more rural environment. He originally purchased and renovated a cottage in Warwick but quickly outgrew it. In 2009, he noticed a For Sale sign on a house on the western side of town and signed the contract within a week. Clint was drawn to the home, which had been built in 1908 — "It had beautiful bones," he says — and named the property The Laurels in honour of its towering camphor laurels.

The house stands on half a hectare and, with its sheds and backyard, made a good location for Clint's landscape business and online retail outlet, The Garden Tool Shop.

Clint's first task was to transform the front garden into an inviting space for visitors. He removed the patchy lawn, which was struggling beneath the trees, and stabilised the sloping block with a terrace. A large fountain went in the centre, circled with a hedge of Japanese box and white 'Iceberg' roses. *Magnolia grandiflora* 'Little Gem' trees flank the house, which Clint has rejuvenated with a coat of white paint.

He worked out the basic design for the garden in the first three months and refined it over time. The result is a series of rooms in varying styles that flow seamlessly from one to the next. Hedges and cones of box-leaved privet (*Ligustrum undulatum*) provide form, while perennial borders are organised according to their colour and watering requirements.

"It's a display of my work and a showcase of plants that do well in the Warwick climate," Clint explains. "It has formal elements and I've used some unconventional plants, especially old-fashioned species. Salvias and penstemon do well here, and I like agastache, dahlias, variegated sedum, miscanthus and rare sunflowers such as 'Moulin Rouge' and 'Lemon Queen'."

Just outside the kitchen window was the obvious spot for the vegetable garden. "I like it to be in a high-traffic area so I can weed and check it regularly," he says. Beyond is a large outdoor dining section that leads to the office. "I love looking out while I work," he says of the view of the garden, which is framed by a pair of French doors that he picked up for a few dollars at a garage sale.

"I believe in using what you have to reduce your carbon footprint, and in finding materials that fit comfortably into their surrounds," Clint says. "Local products have a sense of place and are good for the community. I also try to recycle materials such as the ironbark beams of the arbour, which came from a nearby schoolhouse. I like things that aren't perfect, as they tell a story."

The western side of the property has been transformed into a woodland area, with tropical birches to shade the house during summer and filter sunlight in winter.

Clint has opened The Laurels twice as part of the Open Gardens Australia scheme, and visitors are always drawn to the tree house in a camphor laurel and the cottage-style henhouse in the backyard. "My mother is scared of chooks, so I had to build a pen where she could collect the eggs without going inside," he says, referring to the doors of the nesting boxes that allow access from the outside.

With severe winters and hot, dry summers, Warwick's climate can be harsh on gardens, but Clint has embraced the challenge and focuses on other benefits. "I love the town's sense of community," he says. "I go through three sets of traffic lights to get to the other side of town and in peak hour it only takes three minutes!"

Magnificent wisteria draped over a strong supporting arcade makes a dazzling late-spring display in this Cobbitty garden.

PURPLE REIGN

INSPIRED BY AN ENGLISH ROYAL GARDEN, THIS
SPECTACULAR LAYOUT ON SYDNEY'S RURAL EDGE
SALUTES THE FORMAL GEOMETRIES OF PAST CENTURIES.

Weeping mulberries stand tall behind a *Rhaphiolepis indica* hedge in bloom; the vivid purple shrub is *Loropetalum chinense*.

Curved beds of trees and shrubs guide the view across the lawn. FACING PAGE, CLOCKWISE, FROM TOP LEFT White flowers of *Rhaphiolepis indica*; a quiet corner in the midst of stately living walls; magnolias thrive; shaped shrubs and hedges are intrinsic to this garden's conception.

Inside the squares of the knot garden, white quartz chippings are used as a foil for the green hedges. The yellow hedging is golden privet.

Nola Tegel's studio is almost hidden, carefully camouflaged by trees and shrubs. However, Nola's time spent with paint and brush, both at the easel and outdoors, has had a prominent impact on her gardening life. "I'm more aware of colour, and colour combinations, than I was when I started," she says.

The garden that she and husband Max have created at Cobbitty, on Sydney's southern rural fringe, is more than four hectares of beautifully maintained landscape — sweeping lawns, shapely trees, flower borders and a superb vegetable garden. And the show stopper is the wisteria, planted in 2002 and now a magnificent sight as it drips purple blooms over a supporting arcade. The romantic informality of the overhanging wisteria contrasts with the precise lines of the clipped hedges edging the walkway beneath.

While Max (according to Nola) likes constancy in the garden, and immaculate hedges and lawns, she is all for experimenting with flowers' form and colour. At first, a long border near the driveway was planted in hot colours — vivid reds and pinks with some clashing orange tones. Then Nola envisaged a totally green border. "That looked fine when you were close to it — but standing back, all the plants just blurred together in a mass of green. It wasn't particularly pretty."

So her painterly eye moved on. "Now I'm trying to master a perennial border," she says. "I do like the idea of anticipation and looking forward to each successive wave of blooms. Certain plants that I've used do really well in this climate. Artichokes look fantastic with their silver foliage. The yellow fluffy heads of fennel are a great contrast, and I love the pink tassels of amaranthus. There are even a few survivors of the green border idea mixed with 'Green Goddess' lilies, some agapanthus and the lovely white hydrangea 'Annabelle'.

"In summary, I'm trying to create a border that has interest from spring to autumn. I'm aiming for a great crescendo of colour sometime in the summer … When this happens," Nola says, laughing, "I'll give you a ring!"

She is now confident about her planting and design changes, having learnt by trial and error the best choices for the Cobbitty area. "I made two big mistakes soon after we built the house in 1987 — the first was that I studied garden books and didn't look around me to see which plants did well locally. I was too busy thinking about the flowers I wanted to grow. And I should have thought about the trees and shrubs before flowers. Flowers should have been the last on the list.

"The second mistake was not improving the soil. We're on terrible clay here and I've worked out that for every dollar you spend on plants, you need to spend five times as much on soil improvement. You reap the benefit of that work in the end. But they are hard lessons to learn."

Another example of Nola's pragmatic changes was an early rose layout. When it failed to thrive, she replaced it with an elaborate knot garden. "We were forever spraying the roses for some disease or other, and it just seemed wrong for the environment," she says. "So I've copied some of the design of the knot garden I saw at Hampton Court Palace." Knot gardens — a very formal geometric style of planting — date back to Elizabethan times, although the example at London's Hampton Court was designed in the 1920s. "We've used box, santolina and lavender, and repeated some of the plantings in the area near the vegetable garden with bay trees in big square pots and cones of box."

On the other hand, magnolias — an early gift from family for the then-new garden — absolutely thrive in the area. So, too, do weeping mulberries and hedges of white-flowered Indian hawthorn, *Rhaphiolepis indica*.

Nola has travelled extensively and visited many gardens, but still cites Vita Sackville-West's famous garden at England's Sissinghurst Castle as the one that taught her how to break up spaces in a landscape. "It was an example of how to divide and conquer," she says.

The Tegels are fortunate that their neighbours' large dam makes a beautiful 'borrowed landscape' beyond the sweeping lawns. "I like the sense of continuity as the garden flows into the surrounding paddocks," Nola says. "You have to be careful about the style of trees you plant — the Chinese elms are shady and spreading, and they can be left to grow naturally without severe pruning. You don't want a suburban look …"

As we take our leave, Nora remarks, "Painting makes you aware how to enhance a landscape." Although she has stressed that the first lesson is soil preparation and the second is to plant for your climate, Nola adds that the overarching design principle is to relate the garden to the larger landscape.

Turritable Creek runs down off the mountain through Dreamthorpe, where bridges connect mossy paths in the woodland.

take to the hills
FIELDS OF BULBS HERALD SPRING IN THIS
MOUNTAIN GARDEN NORTH OF MELBOURNE.

Spring beauties. FACING PAGE Transforming the gravel car park into small flower and vegetable plots was one of the owners' major changes.

Planted in the early 1900s, Dreamthorpe's ethereal woodland area is covered in a blanket of bluebells in late October each year.

The planting of deciduous trees, leaves just emerging, allows the sun to penetrate to the forest floor, highlighting bluebells and epimediums.

Dreamthorpe is one of the renowned gardens of Mount Macedon in Victoria. In the late-Victorian and Edwardian eras, grand houses and gardens such as Dreamthorpe were set behind hedges with sweeping lawns and carefully chosen deciduous trees. In the quiet gullies, ponds and lakes were formed, rustic bridges and gazebos built, spring bulbs planted en masse, and rhododendrons mingled with native tree ferns to form shady, mysterious gardens.

Dreamthorpe was first planted by Nat Ronalds in the 1880s as part of the nursery business that provided flowers and foliage for his Melbourne florist shop. But it was Alice Hodges, wife of a judge, Sir Henry Hodges, who established much of the present layout. She lived there from 1902 until 1942 and employed up to 17 garden staff. Many of the significant plants in the garden are from Ronalds's nursery or from Lady Hodges's time.

The present custodians of Dreamthorpe are Jan and Peter Clark, who bought the property in 2003. They say the influence of two major figures in late 19th-century English gardening, William Robinson and Gertrude Jekyll, is clearly evident and that their writings inspired Alice's design and plant choices. Jan cites a passage from Jekyll's *Wood and Garden*: "The large lawn space I am supposing stretches away a good distance from the house and is bounded on the south-west by fine trees: away beyond all of that is wild wood. On summer afternoons the greater part of the lawn is in cool shade, while the winter sun shows through the tree stems."

As Jan points out, it's an almost exact description of Dreamthorpe. "This woodland garden has a unique place in Australian gardening," she says. "To wander its meandering paths is to be transported by its beauty and the peacefulness of a bygone age." It reflects, too, the contemporary aesthetic of woodland gardening and a love of plants brought back from the Orient, which were so popular in England at the time.

From early August until the end of October, the woodland is carpeted with a progression of bulbs — crocus, cyclamens, hellebores, jonquils, daffodils and bluebells. "The entire spring is like an orchestra tuning up and the final crescendo is the vast spread of the bluebells," Jan says. Large trees, including pin oaks (*Quercus palustris*) and Japanese maples (*Acer palmatum*), spread a dense canopy over the paths and mossy steps.

Adding to the cool atmosphere is the tiny Turritable Creek, which trickles and, after heavy rain, hurtles through the garden. Coming from high on the mountain, the stream passes through many of the area's gardens before it enters Dreamthorpe. A lake, almost hidden in the greenery, and a pond, a focus at the end of the main lawn, make the scene extremely picturesque.

In its 130-year history, only a few people have owned Dreamthorpe — and "most of them have been keen gardeners who modified and enhanced the glorious and tranquil garden we have today," Jan says.

The Clarks, too, have made changes and these have certainly enhanced the garden. "We've had a go at everything," Jan says. "Our modifications include slight changes to the curving driveway, rerouting paths, removing many large holly trees, a huge amount of new planting and flowerbeds. We also redesigned the house lawn and the rose trellis to enlarge the view from the front door and terrace — this way we can see the reflecting pond in the oak lawn more clearly."

It's here on this spreading lawn that Alice Hodges used to hold her garden events to celebrate Armistice Day or raise funds for the Red Cross. A bank of white rhododendrons, superb in spring, edges this lawn and separates it from the woodland beyond.

Yet another area that has been sympathetically renovated is the rose circle, redesigned and underplanted with lavender and catmint. The original lilac circle has gone, but its replacement still offers the romantic ambiance of its predecessor. The orchard, too, has had a makeover; some of the trees, planted by Nat Ronalds more than 100 years ago, supplied the people of Mount Macedon with fresh fruit.

The gravel car park has been transformed into a series of small gardens for flowers and vegetables. This change followed a trip to Iran, during which Jan says she became fascinated by Islamic gardens with their fountains, flowers and fruit trees.

The Clarks' renovations and additions are so subtle they have barely disturbed the ethos of this magical garden. At last count, Peter says, there are 28 established places to sit in the garden. "Whatever the weather, you will find a place to go," he says. There's always a sheltered spot to contemplate the distinctive spaces at Dreamthorpe, each with their seasonal period of glory.

golden moments

THE GLORY OF AUTUMN AND A WELCOME
SIGN THAT SPRING IS ON ITS WAY, YELLOW
IS A COLOUR TO CELEBRATE IN THE GARDEN.

SLEEPING BEAUTY

A MAGICAL TASMANIAN GARDEN BEGUN IN THE 1840s
CAPTIVATES WITH ITS EVOCATION OF ENGLISH PARKLAND.

The lake at Culzean in Westbury reflects a parade of trees including lipstick maple, swamp cypress and dawn redwood.

An Indian bean tree (*Catalpa bignonioides*) and a copper beech (*Fagus sylvatica*) guard the patio. FACING PAGE In the dell, a statue is almost hidden among the rhododendrons.

Swamp cypress (*Taxodium distichum*) is reflected in the water. FACING PAGE, CLOCKWISE, FROM TOP LEFT More plantings of hydrangeas are planned for the garden; an inviting bench from which to enjoy the view; 'Iceberg' roses flower late; a huge pin oak dominates the view across the lake.

A pair of lindens (*Tilia cordata*) in Culzean's driveway avenue were planted in the 1870s.

Part of the allure of old gardens is the ambience that only layers of time and the hands of successive custodians can bestow. Culzean at Westbury in Tasmania's north is such a property. Laid out in the 1840s, Culzean was purchased in 2012 by two Launceston dentists: Dinah FitzGerald and her husband, Philip Leith. They were enchanted by the four hectares of shady woodland, lawn and shrubberies encircling a large ornamental lake.

"I wanted to live in the country, and we came and had a look and I just fell in love," Dinah says. "It was the English woodland garden that I so admired, and the trees are just so wonderful — some of the old ones in the dell are original. The lake dominates the garden and that makes it so special. And with Launceston only a half-hour drive away, it worked for us."

Woodbine Cottage was a 16-hectare farm settled in 1842 by a former officer in the Indian army. Over the years, he established the garden with a sweeping circular drive in front of the house and a small valley of oaks, elms and other exotic trees.

Many other owners followed — "It was often a place where people came to retire," explains Dinah — and more planting. For example, in the 1870s a driveway avenue of lindens, golden ashes, copper beeches and sequoia was established. And there were further name changes. At different times it was called Blair Athol, Leicesterville and finally Culzean, after Culzean Castle on the west coast of Scotland.

From 1965 until 2000, veterinarian Harry Laker ran a small nursery at Culzean. "Laker is acknowledged as the person who put the main structure into the garden and built the lake, which supposedly has an island in the shape of Tasmania with a pin oak in the centre," Dinah says.

Laker's particular penchant was for roses — " 'Apricot Nectar' and 'Icebergs' were his thing" — which he sold in the nursery. But he also planted many trees, including conifers and the American *Catalpa bignonioides*, along with banks of azaleas and rhododendrons. At the lake he put in thousands of waterlilies and ringed it with yellow water iris (*Iris pseudacorus*). It makes for a truly spectacular sight in spring, although they are now so abundant that they need drastic thinning.

Culzean was in fine shape when Dinah and Philip took over. "The house was in beautiful order, and the garden was well maintained and had a watering system and excellent infrastructure," Dinah says. "My plan was not to do anything for a year, just to maintain and watch.

"Then we had the delight in spring of walking around, discovering everything. There were all kinds of bulbs and *Cyclamen persicum*, and a mass of trout lilies …"

And with the garden having yielded up its secrets through a yearly cycle, Dinah is now embarking on the next stage of its evolution. "I think what I'd like to achieve is more interest at ground level. I'd like to have masses of American woodland plants, like aruncus and dogwood, and some fritillaria."

A walk meanders around the lake through stands of magnificent trees, including copper beech (*Fagus sylvatica*), swamp cypress (*Taxodium distichum*), *Sequoia sempervirens* and an evergreen holm oak (*Quercus ilex*). In late autumn their reflections glow in the water. "The lake is fed by a creek that comes in as a tributary of Quamby Brook," Dinah says. "We have platypus but no fish because of the eels."

Regardless of the season, there's always a particular specimen to admire, such as a towering maritime pine (*Pinus pinaster*) with its graceful long needles. Further on is the woodland that Dinah finds so enchanting. "This is a favourite area because I love the view of the house and lake from here."

Culzean is a pleasure garden in all seasons, thanks to the foresight and nurturing of owners past and present. Now Dinah and Philip's passion for the garden will ensure it continues into the future.

"Philip will come home from work and walk around the garden with the dog and a glass of wine," she says. "When I walk, I usually have a mission, and I'll stop and think and plan. I have days here by myself that are lovely. I don't think I'll ever fall out of love with this garden."

temple to nature

A MAGNIFICENT HILLSIDE GARDEN NORTH
OF MELBOURNE, THE LEGACY OF MANY OWNERS,
CONTAINS CHARMING REFERENCES TO ANTIQUITY.

The Temple of the Winds, a beautiful folly in this Macedon Ranges garden, was modelled on a similar structure in Melbourne's Royal Botanic Gardens.

CLOCKWISE, FROM TOP LEFT Gladwin iris (*Iris foetidissima*); the house seen beyond a bed of box hedging, snowdrops and hellebores; trees like this Japanese maple are owner Ann Coughlan's favourites; a seal fountain. FACING PAGE Waterlilies on the old swimming pool known as the Roman Baths.

"Our hellebores are a signature plant for colder climates," says Ann of plantings such as *Helleborus purpureus*. FACING PAGE Lenten rose (*Helleborus orientalis*) carpets the ground.

The formal potager, defined by clipped box and enclosed by holly and laurel hedges, has been replanted and is Ann's pride and joy.

FACING PAGE Stone stairs and terraces were part of the landscaping done by a previous owner in the early 1930s.

During the late 19th and early 20th centuries, Mount Macedon was a fashionable summer retreat for many of Melbourne's establishment families. They came for the cooler climate and fresh mountain air, and emulated the style of colonial Indian hill stations, building stately homes and planting gardens with collections of rare plants and trees.

"Gentlemen came here as a retreat and competed to grow the rarest species," says Steve Coughlan, who, with his wife, Ann, owns Cameron Lodge, one of the oldest and most important gardens in the Macedon Ranges, less than an hour's drive north of Melbourne. "Cameron Lodge has had many owners and I would say each one has had a different interest. One gent collected holly while another had fir and spruce, and another had camellias."

When Steve and Ann bought the property in late 2011 and moved from Melbourne, their wish list had included a place with history, proximity to the city for commuting — Steve is in telecommunications and Ann works for an energy company — and a garden.

Their first view was online, but Cameron Lodge seemed to tick all the boxes. "The trees were out in their autumn glory, the village pub had just reopened, I could be home quickly," Ann says. "I didn't want to look at the house, just the garden ..." Steve adds, "And within five minutes of walking through, we were sold."

What they had discovered was a magical parkland of sweeping lawns and clipped hedges, with dark towering conifers and glowing deciduous trees shading banks of hydrangeas, azaleas and rhododendrons. A series of stone terraces and stairs, and formal structures such as the Summer Pergola — a pillared walk dripping in wisteria — enticed them onto the lower level where a stream, Turritable Creek, bubbled down the mountain.

Here they found the relics of a more flamboyant era. There was the Roman Baths, an old concrete swimming pool in a classical design (now dotted with buttery yellow waterlilies) and the Temple of the Winds, another inspiration from antiquity, set on a tiny island.

Overlooking it all was the Indian colonial-style house built in 1886 by Edward Woods. He named it Rahiri, but in 1916 it was renamed Cameron Lodge by the next owner, William Cameron. As the director of British American Tobacco, Cameron had the means and opportunity to develop the garden. He built the stone terraces and, in 1932, commissioned garden designer Joan Anderson to plan the Temple of the Winds, modelled on a similar structure in Melbourne's Royal Botanic Gardens. However, this version has more romance, as you can reach it only by crossing a lily pond on stepping stones shaped like elephants' feet. In the pond, copper statues of elephants and seals hold fountains.

"Cameron used to come here with his mates to play cards, and the butler would bring the drinks on the tray," Steve says. "We've got a four-wheel-drive with a tray on the back, so we'll come here with a sixpack of beer and a bag of firelighters," he adds, laughing at the comparison.

He and Ann cut back lanky azaleas and hydrangeas, and restored the pergola's pillars, and the stone steps and terraces. However, during the first year they mostly waited for the garden to reveal itself. "Our intention is to bring it back to the original design, and to clear the view so you can see the various rooms," Steve says.

Each of them perceives special magic in different ways. For Steve, it's the gnarled winter skeleton of a weeping elm, looking up into the radiating branches of an awesome giant redwood (*Sequoiadendron giganteum*) and the vistas across the sweeping lawns.

Ann loves the magnificence of the Northern Hemisphere trees, especially in autumn. "We first saw it in autumn and winter, and could see then how diverse it would be and how it would change," Steve says. "We have an autumn walk with a string of maples and beeches ... They're underplanted with hellebores, and in winter it's spectacular all through the garden."

They enjoy sharing the beauty of the garden with others, and in spring and autumn they invite visitors via Open Gardens Australia. Guests who stay in their refurbished bed-and-breakfast cottage are encouraged to wander in the garden.

While they work towards William Cameron's original vision, Ann and Steve don't aspire to being able to enjoy it in his extravagant style, let alone break out the playing cards. "I always promise myself I'll come down to the temple with a bottle of wine, and a book and a chair, but it hasn't happened yet," Steve says.

"The restoration will be ongoing, but our ethos is more of a natural garden. We like trimmed bushes, but we also like to see the garden look like it's always been there. We certainly wanted that touch with history."

The parterre garden with catmint, lavender, 'Jane McGrath' roses and Chinese crabapples. FACING PAGE Lombardy poplars line the driveway.

the high life

HIGH ON THE MONARO
PLAINS, A STRIKING
SUBALPINE GARDEN BUILDS
ON THREE GENERATIONS
OF DEDICATED PLANTING.

Lombardy poplars, basket willows and a cypress line the shore. FACING PAGE A former pumphouse is now dubbed the 'boathouse'.

A beautiful stone wall by a group of gleditsias, planted for their brilliant yellow foliage in autumn.

A silver poplar (*Populus alba*) shelters grazing sheep. FACING PAGE, CLOCKWISE, FROM TOP LEFT Vinca is a hardy ground cover; most of the trees were planted by John's grandfather; catmint in flower; Sally-Ann passes a Himalayan cypress on a shaded path.

A planting of pin oaks has matured to create a shady, quiet corner in the garden.

Entering the long driveway that leads to the homestead, you are greeted by towering poplars, perfectly manicured gardens and a lake that suggests the north of Italy rather than the Monaro Plains of south-east NSW.

Shirley, a grazing property some 10 kilometres south of the village of Nimmitabel, is an anomaly in the Monaro landscape, due to its high altitude, significantly cooler climate and above-average rainfall. "We're about 1000 metres above sea level with a subalpine climate," says owner John Cottle. "We have late frosts and falls of snow up to a metre deep, which certainly bring their share of challenges to the garden."

John and his wife, Sally-Ann, took over the family-owned property in 1997, moving here with their two children, Georgina and Harrison (now in their 20s). John oversees the running of the 1400-hectare sheep and cattle station while finding time to tend to his real passion, the garden.

"The garden was established by my grandparents, who purchased the property in 1935," he says. "They were the perfect team, as George would plant trees while Anne looked after the rest of the garden."

One striking result of this early involvement is the stands of trees — cedars, sequoias, pines, spruces, elms, birches and chestnuts — that have thrived in the cool climate.

Work stalled during World War II but was enthusiastically resumed in 1946 with the construction of the lake and island. The many flowerbeds, filled with annuals and perennials, continued to expand with the addition of a sunken garden. Some beautifully detailed stonework was constructed next to the lake by an English stonemason from nearby Bombala.

In the 1960s, the garden was inherited by John's mother, Joy, with her husband, Geoffrey Cottle. On her return to Shirley, Joy reorganised the garden so that she could maintain it without having to rely on staff. Many of the labour-intensive flowerbeds were removed and replaced with shrubs, ground cover and trees to create more of a park-like landscape.

"My mother was the second generation in our family to develop this passion for gardening, and she truly devoted herself to this property," John says. The garden thrived under Joy's guardianship and she oversaw the installation of a watering system, a major improvement.

"When we came to live here, the garden had already been included in many open days, including those for the Garden History Society, the Australian Club and the Commonwealth Club, as well as numerous local events and fundraisers," John says. "We knew we were taking on quite a responsibility and we recognised that we would need professional help if we were to make changes in the future."

John and Sally-Ann had long admired the work of Melbourne landscape designer Paul Bangay, and in 2006 they began redesigning the garden to Bangay's master plan. "Paul introduced structure with extensive plantings of hedges that helped to define particular areas," John says. "This changed the garden, giving it a more formal feel."

The garden was also extended to include the back of the homestead. A large paved courtyard, crabapple lawn and parterre garden have replaced the old tennis court.

John has worked hard to implement Paul's plans, which enhanced his mother's and his grandparents' original designs. And influenced by the work of some modern European garden designers — in particular, Jacques Wirtz from Belgium and the Spaniard Fernando Caruncho — John has ambitions for future paddock plantings that will be striking 'living' artworks.

Meanwhile, reflecting on his years of work, John says, "I hope this garden will continue to bring joy to the many that come to see it and in turn always be cared for by the generations to come."

Daffodils in flower at Bark Ridge. FACING PAGE Karingal is another private garden that will be full of daffodils in September.

FESTIVAL OF GOLD

SPRING MEANS JUST ONE THING IN A NSW CENTRAL WEST VILLAGE — A FAMOUS BURST OF DAFFODILS THAT BRINGS VISITORS FROM FAR AND WIDE.

CLOCKWISE, FROM
TOP LEFT 'Ice Follies'
at Bark Ridge; the 1860s
cottage at Karingal;
massed plantings of
'Grand Monarque' at
Bark Ridge; daffodils
feature in many local
gardens. FACING PAGE
Daffodils planted right
to the fence lines
at Bark Ridge.

Wordsworth, who put daffodils at the heart of one of his most famous poems, would have loved the tiny village of Rydal on the western side of NSW's Blue Mountains. Every September, hosts of golden daffodils don't just dance beside the lake and beneath the trees. They also toss their heads beside the police station, around the schoolhouse, past the church and up towards the pub. They even stretch along the railway line.

The village was named Rydal in 1843 after the hamlet in England's Lake District where William Wordsworth lived from 1813 until his death in 1850. Visitors wandering through the four private gardens and the village grounds during the Daffodils at Rydal festival will easily equal the "Ten thousand saw I at a glance" that Wordsworth celebrated in 'I Wandered Lonely as a Cloud'. In fact, they're likely to see more than 100,000 blooms.

"They just bring people so much joy," says Lindsay Green, one of the festival organisers. "They come to see the daffodils, but it's also very social. Old friends catch up and families have reunions. I think I must have met everyone's mother, brother, cousin, best friend and aunty.

"Sometimes people are yarning away in our shed over a cup of tea for hours."

It's about five degrees the day we arrive, but already thousands of green shoots are peeping up through the frosty paddocks. Laurie and Lindsay have lit their wood fire inside their cottage on their 80-hectare property, Bark Ridge. As Lindsay makes tea — served in teacups and saucers decorated with daffodils — it's easy to see what attracted them to the place.

Spread beyond their living room, rolling away towards the horizon, are gentle hills interspersed with swathes of bush. "It's incredibly beautiful, isn't it?" Laurie remarks.

When they bought the property back in 1987, they found about 30 daffodils flourishing and, in a classic understatement, "decided to plant some more". They began using a plough, drawn by a truck, to plant the bulbs each year. Now they simply throw the bulbs on the ground and cover them with soil.

Daffodils had long been grown in Rydal, but in 2002 an association was formed, the festival was launched and planting began in earnest. As word spread, and more and more of the villagers planted beds of daffodils, the visitor numbers began to grow steadily each September.

"The atmosphere is wonderful," Lindsay says. "Artists are setting up their easels, photographers are clicking away and bands are playing." Children love it because there's a surprise around every corner. Also worth a visit are the private gardens of Chapel House, the former home of artist John Olsen, and Karingal, both of which are not far from the village.

Such is the attraction of the festival that Laurie has a friend who organises his annual business trips from Germany around the two September weekends.

Garden clubs and walking groups often book bus tours during the week. Although, as Laurie warns, make sure you get the dates right. "We've had tours that arrive, and everyone clambers out of the bus and says, 'Oh, where are they?'"

Anne Krone, who owns Rydal Mount, the former schoolhouse named after Wordswotrth's own home, says it's a poignant time; her partner, John Wellings, died during the 2006 festival. "The event was always an amazing dream of his, so I just filled the house and church with bulbs," she says.

In past years more than 1600 people have visited Rydal to immerse themselves in daffodils. "Not bad for a village of 80, is it?" Anne says. The Rydal Village Association has raised more than $90,000 for nursing homes and respite centres for families with special needs.

"Sharing the gardens gives us as much pleasure as the work involved," Lindsay says. "We love the beautiful cards and letters from people saying how much they enjoyed the weekend."

The village has plans to plant even more daffodils; the residents aim to line the five-kilometre road that leads from the village to the highway. It will be hard to leave the place without feeling cheerful.

our favourites

FROM HEIRLOOM VARIETIES TO
THE UNRULY BEAUTY OF AUSTRALIAN
NATIVES, THE PLANTS AND IDEAS IN
THESE GARDENS WILL INSPIRE.

The vibrant coloured *Sedum* 'Autumn Joy' in front of the wisteria-draped sandstone cottage.

fruits of the erth

VICTORIA'S FAMOUS GARDEN AT ST ERTH,
ESTEEMED FOR ITS BEAUTY AND ITS PRODUCE,
GOES FROM STRENGTH TO STRENGTH.

Yellow coneflower
(*Echinacea paradoxa*);
FACING PAGE The
distinctive blue flowers of
Russian sage with seaside
daisies and common sage.

CLOCKWISE, FROM TOP LEFT Vegetable garden gate; autumn crocus (*Colchicum autumnale*); some kangaroo statues; pineapple lily (*Eucomis bicolour*). FACING PAGE Flax and zebra grass contrast with silvery lamb's ear and *Artemisia* 'Powis Castle'.

A view out to the garden from the cottage built in the 1860s by goldminer Matthew Rogers.

Nuggets of gold are rarely found these days at the Garden of St Erth. Any golden lumps lying around are much more likely to be fat pumpkins hiding under their large, floppy leaves. Flowers, fruit and vegetables are the present-day bounty to be won from the earth in this peaceful nursery and garden in Victoria's central highlands, around 90 kilometres north-west of Melbourne.

A simple sandstone cottage, dating from the early 1860s, is the focal point of the garden. It was built by a successful goldminer (and former stonemason), Matthew Rogers, who named his Australian home after the Cornish village in which he was born. It sits alongside the garden's central axis that, in turn, parallels the main road of the once-bustling town of Simmons Reef which, during the 1850s goldrush, attracted up to 10,000 inhabitants.

From 1973, Tommy and Penny Garnett, and other family members, created the famous garden where they grew plants originating from all corners of the globe. In 1980, St Erth was one of Australia's first private gardens opened to the public. Tommy, a former headmaster of Geelong Grammar School, had found time to further his lifelong passion for gardening. He wrote: "At my retirement, my colleagues wished to buy me a present … it was a deodar, a weeping mulberry, a tulip tree, a gingko and a dawn redwood."

Clive Blazey, the founder of the mail-order company Diggers Seeds and one of Garnett's former students, took over the garden in 1996. (It's now managed by the Diggers Garden and Environmental Trust.)

"Tommy and Penny had been advised that the area was unsuitable for gardening — yet they carried on in indomitable fashion to create one of Victoria's finest gardens," Clive recalls. On a recent return visit to the property, Penny Garnett recalled how she and Tommy often left Geelong for weekends at St Erth with trailer-loads of horse manure to improve the soil.

Today, visitors in autumn enjoy an extensive range of perennials, including richly coloured dahlias and salvias, contrasting with bold clumps of ornamental grasses such as miscanthus and panicum. In spring, the legacy of Tommy's daffodil plantings bursts forth in bright yellow splashes that contrast vividly with the darker shades of the surrounding Wombat State Forest. As summer approaches, the blooms of some exquisite cool-climate plants that can be grown in only a few places in Australia — such as Himalayan blue poppies (*Meconopsis betonicifolia*) — are a spectacular sight.

In the latest developments, the old orchard has been revitalised with espaliered rows of apples, pears, quinces, cherries and plums. What Clive calls a "food forest" of fruit-yielding shrubs and ground covers — including blackcurrants, strawberries and rhubarb — has also been planted to showcase Clive's idea of an "Eden in your backyard" that integrates food and flowers.

Clive believes that a life of quality begins at the table and he has replaced some plants with more productive varieties. It's all part of the fork-to-fork philosophy that's also intrinsic to Heronswood, the Diggers' headquarters on Victoria's Mornington Peninsula. "Freshness, diversity and taste are the reasons you should grow your own food," Clive says.

For example, he maintains that avocados are so easy to grow that they should be in everyone's backyard. "If you can grow camellias or lemons, you can grow avocados — and other fruits of the future, such as white sapote, Shahtoot mulberry, the Chinese date or the Brazilian tree grape," he enthuses.

However, that appetite for produce doesn't mean neat rows of vegetables with not a flower in sight; far from it. The Garden of St Erth rejoices in being highly visible and is best appreciated when visitors pay attention to its ornamental as well as its productive aspects.

The mingling of colour and form in flowers and vegetables is dramatic. Dark leaves on dahlias are echoed in dark Tuscan kale and 'Bull's Blood' beetroot; pale lime zinnias are exactly the same hue as lettuce leaves. 'Purple King' beans twirling up poles pick up the colour of a nearby salvia flower; bright green parsley makes a decorative edge; and form and foliage are brilliantly combined, from red-leafed lettuces to 'Ruby' brussels sprouts and rainbow chard. All this delicious harvest ends up on plates in the café at St Erth, another attraction that draws visitors.

And when one sees the crowds that flock to St Erth during its twice-yearly festivals — a bold show of perennials and a bountiful harvest of vegetables in autumn, and a stunning display of daffodils and blossoming fruit trees in spring — it's clear this has become one of Victoria's best-loved gardens.

Plantings of kangaroo paw at Passchendaele flower farm. FACING PAGE Cassia Scott and her close friend have a bouquet to deliver.

where the wild things are

FEW THINGS SURPASS THE BEAUTY OF AUSTRALIAN
WILDFLOWERS FOR CRAIG SCOTT, WHO HAS TURNED
HIS PASSION INTO A SUCCESSFUL BUSINESS.

Dorrigo waratah (*Alloxylon pinnatum*). FACING PAGE The dam that feeds the irrigation pipes is also the family swimming hole.

CLOCKWISE, FROM TOP LEFT Sturt's desert pea; the property covers 20 hectares; Angie holds orange kangaroo paw; assorted kangaroo paw varieties. FACING PAGE Being relatively close to the Sydney Flower Market, the Scotts don't need to box their flowers for shipping.

Cassia and Miranda help out by carrying a container of flowering gum blooms. FACING PAGE A dwarf orange gum makes a brilliant morning display.

I t's hot and sunny, and the air on Craig Scott's Mangrove Mountain property is full of the summery drone of bees tasting the flowering gums and hovering over colourful rows of kangaroo paws almost as tall as Craig is.

As he walks through a paddock in the sunshine, each native's display competes for attention. The frilly skirted flowering gums in bright red, orange and pink are offset by russet, pale green or golden kangaroo paws and, down the hill by the property's dam, the high-top blooms of Gymea lilies.

"I really do love it up here," he says. "In the bush you get Christmas bells, waratahs and Gymea lilies just growing naturally. There's so much space, which we all cherish, and my four daughters love swimming in the dam." The 20-hectare property, named Passchendaele by the World War I veteran who was its original owner, is a 40-minute drive west of Gosford on the NSW central coast.

Craig's father, Colin, bought the property in 1968, put in irrigation and the dam, and had dreams of moving up here to live. But then he and Craig's mother, Lois, had second thoughts and stayed at their flower farm at Bangor on Sydney's southern outskirts, not too far from where Craig's great-grandfather once walked through the bush, picking greenery to sell at city markets.

It was Craig — the fourth-generation flower grower — who made the jump beyond Sydney. He decided to move to Passchendaele with Angie after they married in 1988. As they set about raising their daughters — Bethany, Miranda, Eden and Cassia — Craig also established East Coast Wildflowers in partnership with Colin.

The focus at East Coast has always been natives and, apart from the quieter months between late autumn and mid-winter, Craig has plenty in bloom. They include the gums and kangaroo paws, Christmas bush, flannel flowers, Sturt's desert pea, and varieties of waratah and grevillea.

He also has two greenhouses to nurture seedlings, and other weather-sensitive plants, which he coaxes into bloom early in order to beat his rivals to market. The flowers are wrapped in bunches in the farm shed, then taken by van to the Sydney Flower Market at Flemington in the city's western suburbs.

"The beauty of having the farm here is that we're only 70 minutes from the markets," Craig says. "A lot of the other guys have to pack their flowers into boxes and then ship them — and that costs a lot."

However, one inescapable downside to a market-driven business is that three days a week Craig typically works a 12-hour day, starting at about midnight, in order to get his flowers to the buyers.

"It *is* hard work," he concedes, "but I really do enjoy growing something that's lovely and uniquely Australian. That's a great thing. And also, when the florists get your flowers and you get direct feedback from them or their satisfied customers, that's great, too."

The popularity of native flowers has grown steadily, particularly as fresh varieties became available. The word from Craig's customers, including major florists such as Grandiflora, is that Australians now have a greater appreciation of natives' beauty and lasting nature, their ability to thrive in an often-harsh climate and the contrast between delicate and sculptural elements in a display.

Craig is particularly pleased to see his wildflowers reach a wider audience, as occurred when they were used in staircase displays in the Sydney Opera House during the 2007 APEC summit or at the 2009 Christmas celebration at NSW's Government House.

"It's just lovely to have flora that is uniquely our own," he says. "The seasonality of the flowers keeps it exciting and interesting, because they're always fresh, and people look forward to them each year. I say they should be cherished." He laughs and adds, "People think I get a bit carried away at times."

Despite the Scotts' love for their farm, they have made the tough decision to shift the family base to Somersby. It's about halfway between the farm and Gosford, where Angie works as an art teacher.

Craig acknowledges the wrench each time he comes back to Passchendaele, but adds the many trips to and from Gosford, particularly on weekends to fit in with the girls' activities, had become too wearing on them all. Now a visit to the property turns into a swimming expedition, or simply an excuse to see the place again.

"Once you move away you do become a bit detached," he says. "But it's lovely driving through the front gate and seeing the view across the front lawn to the dam. Dad still comes up every week, too."

Don Schofield has nurtured his two-hectare garden in Mount Tomah since 1979. Tulips, 'Warley Rose' and dianthus are in profusion.

NEVER-ENDING STORY

WITH A PLOT HERE AND A STRIP THERE, THIS GARDEN IN THE
NSW BLUE MOUNTAINS HAS GROWN FROM SMALL TO GRAND.

CLOCKWISE, FROM
TOP LEFT Don has an
outstanding collection
of hydrangeas; the rock
garden at the top of the
property; a budding

rhododendron; hedging
leads down to the
woodland plantings.
FACING PAGE
American dogwood,
'Cherokee Chief'.

Blue lupins and 'Blushing
Beauty'. FACING PAGE
Against a background of
conifers and shrubs, this
parterre layout makes
good use of some flat land.

Kurume azaleas along
a path are another feature
of Don's beautiful property.

The call of a whipbird snaps through the tallest branches of Don Schofield's Blue Mountains garden as he winds his way down paths that follow the land's natural contours. With every step, more surprising plants, shapes and colours come into view. Whatever you expect, this is even more spectacular.

For more than 30 years Don has amassed the rare and heritage varieties that grace Winterwood. He created this two-hectare garden at Mount Tomah from nothing, tending it with a fine eye for detail ever since it was razed by a bushfire three days after he bought it in 1979.

His love of plants is clear. Stopping occasionally, he bends to cup a flower's face, turning it up to be seen. He refers to the plants fondly, like favourite family members.

"She's a lovely thing," he says, pointing out 'Molly the Witch', otherwise known as *Paeonia mlokosewitschii* or golden peony. "Here's one that's finished, this straggly little thing. Hello, little chap." And on he goes.

From the top of the garden, he looks down through the thick, dark foliage. A ghostly pink tree flickers into sight, strangely pale and striking. Don explains that it's a *Cedrela sinensis*, related to the Australian red cedar, and it appears in this colour only in cooler climates.

His plan when he first came here was to have a small garden and let the rest of the property return to bush. Gradually, though, he added another little strip of garden, then another and another until he reached what he decided would be the cut-off point halfway down the hill. "I was definitely not going further than about here," he says, stopping near a cedar that had been transferred from a pot to the garden by the previous owner.

In fact Don has extended the garden twice as far again. He says there's a degree of madness behind this inability to stop — he thinks it comes with the elevation. "I got to the bottom and it was too good not to use because it was level — it had been ploughed for potatoes in the '60s. And the middle bit just looked silly if I didn't neaten it up."

Certainly no part of the garden looks silly now. From the bed of heather at the highest point, past a collection of hostas of many varieties, pincushion-shaped dianthus, a gnarled weeping cherry that shelters a frog pond, and right down to the vivid peonies at the bottom of the garden, there is much to interest the eye. Myriad maples, rampant rhododendrons, delightful dogwoods, pretty paper daisies ... the alliterative list stretches out before you.

The flat section at the bottom of the hill contains some whimsical garden art in the form of a sensuously curving box parterre that looks like it might spin like a top, and a cheeky topiary caterpillar, also box. Another outstanding plant is the monkey puzzle tree in the heart of the garden — a rarity in Australia, says Don, because the seeds aren't available here. He has three of them, grown from New Zealand seeds.

Don inherited an extensive collection of heritage hydrangeas assembled by his friend Joan Arnold, whose Buskers End was one of the outstanding gardens of the NSW Southern Highlands for many years. He brought them to Winterwood as cuttings wrapped in newspaper. They include a group of small, wild hydrangeas and a few climbing varieties. One of them is engaged in a battle with a tree fern beside the path he's following. "I think the hydrangea will win," Don says. "Elsewhere I've given another one a gumtree and said, 'Go your hardest!' "

He has bought seed from plant societies in the UK and swaps plants with other collectors — the tiny Japanese *kurume* azaleas, for example, came from botanist Peter Valder at nearby Mount Wilson. As Don points to them, a yellow robin tinkles unseen above and a little scrubwren skips across the leaf-strewn lawn path. It's quiet and cool and peaceful. You can't help but wonder if Don finds a pleasant corner in which to meditate here occasionally, though opportunities might be limited. He also does gardening work for clients and sells bulbs and cut flowers.

Crunchy, juicy apples have been a highlight. A heavy dust storm in 2010 stole all the flowers from his heritage apple collection — some 22 varieties in all — which enforced a two-year absence from producing fruit. But in 2012, Don reaped a bumper harvest. "It was a triumph — I was taking wheelbarrows of them out in April and still eating my way through them in July," he recalls.

Alongside his bought and inherited collections, Don has bred some plants — including the 'Winterwood Pink' anemone and the 'Winterwood Atkinsii' snowdrop — which have since been released commercially. He is working on a soon-to-be-registered-and-released project. So, no, there's not a lot of time for meditation.

"I go out at the end of the day and try the gardener's trick of one hand tied behind the back while the other is allowed to hold a glass of some kind," he says. Otherwise, this labour of love is never-ending.

inspirations

FROM HEDGING TO ROCKERIES, HERE
ARE SOME PRACTICAL TECHNIQUES THAT
CAN TRANSFORM YOUR OWN GARDEN.

CUTTING EDGE

*A hedge is a line of tightly **growing trees** or shrubs that marks a **boundary** or forms a **screen**. Maintenance is the key. You can opt for a length of **box hedge** with lumps and bumps that imitates an old, overgrown hedge — but still keep it clipped. Or you can choose the **sharp-edged** look that may need clipping **three or four** times a year.*

SUPPORT ACTS

*There are many plants that look
and **perform better** if anchored,
propped or tied to a **support**.
What a shame to see a wisteria
left to run at ground level —
this, of all **climbing plants**,
demands help to get into the air;
in flower, it should be a dripping
sensation, **an ornament** for an
archway or pergola.*

WHITE MAGIC

EXPLORE THE CLASSIC BEAUTY OF THE
ALL-WHITE GARDEN, WHOSE SUBTLE VARIATIONS
ARE OFFSET BY SURROUNDING GREENERY.

CLOCKWISE, FROM TOP LEFT The full and delicate blooms of roses are intrinsic to white gardens; *Viburnum sargentii* 'Onondaga' shows the effective contrast of dark green foliage; 'Seduction' is a popular rose choice; Lord Howe wedding lilies are beautiful and hardy.

All-white schemes are one of the enduring classics of garden design. When perfected, the result is a dazzling array, with interplay between different shapes, sizes and textures of white-on-white flowers. Layers of interest also rely on background foliage of varied texture and form.

This sort of planting can be sustained through the seasons. The best plan is to have a new peak every three or four weeks, built around plants that flower almost continuously. Groundcover plants can range from the smallest spring bulbs — snowdrops if it's cold enough to grow them — and narcissus, through to violas and cushions of *Iberis sempervirens*. Stately agapanthus or Lord Howe wedding lilies (*Dietes robinsoniana*) are almost indestructible. And think of those tough, autumn-flowering bulbs that survive hot summers year after year — nerines and white belladonna lilies.

Annuals can also fit the bill, from alyssum to lobelia. Come the summer, white marigolds, nicotiana, white zinnias and white annual salvia can billow in the beds, but look equally attractive in pots or troughs. Taller annuals — cleome, cosmos, Queen Anne's lace, snapdragons — can soften any harsh corners and help create a romantic mood. With its large sprays of white flowers, the Mexican tree daisy (*Montanoa bipinnatifida*) is great for covering a corner.

The two best complementary colours for background foliage in white gardens are dark green and silver-grey. Classic white flowers can look good in our strong light but are often too harsh on their own. A word of warning: it's possible to have too much white in a dry country garden where the flowers can look dusty and muddy. They need to be backed by a strong green from hedges or trees, or placed against grey walls or trellises that have been painted sage green or grey.

Grey foliage can soften any such overload. Tall branches of grey-green globe artichokes can offer colour support to a magnificent group of *Lilium regale*, or a scramble of white rose or clematis running up the branches of a silver-leaved pear. In a smaller space, combine silver- and grey-leaved herbs, such as santolina or lavender, with white annuals; underplant white roses with silvery lamb's ears (*Stachys byzantina*) or an *Artemisia* 'Powis Castle' or 'Valerie Finnis'.

And what white garden would be complete without a collection of roses? Perfumed and visible long after dusk, there is a wide selection, from the ubiquitous 'Iceberg' and 'Seduction', to sweetly scented David Austin roses such as 'Claire Austin', 'Winchester Cathedral' or 'Glamis Castle'. And it's impossible to ignore great ramblers like 'Rambling Rector', 'Wedding Day' and the wonderful *Rosa brunonii*. White flowers on trees or shrubs with glossy, evergreen foliage are a stand-out. Think gardenias, camellias, choisya or the fabulous *Viburnum sargentii* 'Onondaga' — it's a look that never goes out of fashion.

The most influential of all white gardens was that at Sissinghurst Castle in the UK. Created in the 1930s by Vita Sackville-West and Harold Nicolson, the castle's stunning White Garden has been emulated by gardeners around the world ever since..

The White Garden

• White flowers offer great value for gardeners. They combine happily with any other colour. Yet white also has sufficient impact to stand on its own or to act as a buffer between two colours.

• White also reflects light and therefore lightens the mood. Flowers that like shady conditions, from lily of the valley to rhododendrons, or spring-flowering shrubs, such as viburnums, brighten up areas under trees.

• The brilliance of white means that shapes and patterns of flowers are more intrusive in mixed plantings. Plants with strong silhouettes, such as lilies or camellias, stand out among darker colours. Flowers with a delicate appearance — gaura or thalictrum, for example — create misty effects.

• Green leaves make a dark foil for white flowers. Think of the perfection of the white camellia offset by its leaves. Also consider silver-grey foliage as an elegant backdrop for white flowers; the neutral colours create a sense of calm.

FACING PAGE Use natural elevation or introduce contours to ensure paths can drain after rain.

THE RIGHT PATH

*The type of path you create can be crucial to a **garden's success**. Ideally, you should be able to use it in **all weathers**, particularly during or after rain. A **solid base** is best for paths that are used frequently or if they need to resist **heavy wear**. Materials such as concrete, **paving or stone** create paths that can be walked on even in the **wettest weather**.*

GOING UP THE WALL

Maximise planting by making use of vertical space. This is especially useful in a **productive garden**, where fruiting trees, such as **apples, pears and citrus** — particularly lemons — can be trained as an **espalier**. Choose a tree with a straight stem and most of its branches growing in **one plane**. Plant the tree close to the base of a trellis, fence or wall.

fleeting beauty

AUTUMN IS THE BEST TIME TO GET TULIP BULBS INTO THE
GROUND FOR A BRIEF BUT SPECTACULAR DISPLAY IN SPRING.

White tulips dotted among box plantings. FACING PAGE The splendid show lasts just a few weeks.

Tulips, ancient species or modern hybrids, herald spring's arrival. Their large bell-shaped flowers come in a dazzling array of colours — cream, yellow, orange, pink, red and maroon — and even fringes and stripes. Planted en masse, as they have been in great city gardens for centuries, they are, for many, the brightest jewels.

Long before tulips were known in Europe, the Ottoman sultans planted them by the thousand. After his successful siege of Constantinople in 1453, Mehmed II, a keen gardener, ordered great drifts of bulbs when he built the Topkapi Palace and set out its extensive gardens.

One hundred years later, tulips had become the unofficial emblem of the great imperial city, which by then had been renamed Istanbul. During the reign of Suleiman the Magnificent (1520–66), the tulip emerged as a favourite decorative motif, carved in marble and wood, painted in manuscripts and woven into textiles.

A 16th-century Flemish diplomat, Ogier Ghiselin de Busbecq, is credited with introducing tulip bulbs to Europe. The Low Countries took to the new flower with such enthusiasm that barely a century later they were plunged into the extraordinary 'tulipmania' phenomenon, in which tulip bulbs became the focus of a speculative bubble that rocked the Dutch economy. In 1637, an auction of 99 lots of tulip bulbs in Leiden realised the astounding sum of around $11.25 million in today's currency. Trade took place while bulbs were still in the ground — the buyer had no idea of the actual weight or what the blooms would look like.

Tulips still fascinate, although happily for today's gardeners, prices are nothing like those in the 17th century. For some enthusiasts like botanical artist Diana Everett, unknown species are the lure. "One of the excitements of tulip hunting is finding one that fits no existing description," she says.

In her 2013 book, *The Genus Tulipa: The Tulips of the World* (Botanical Magazine Monograph), she documents some 132 species, most of which she has seen during trips to central Asia. "Life on these trips is very varied," she wrote. "Sometimes the little hotels are comfortable, while others leave much to be desired. We stayed in eastern Kazakhstan in the first week of May. It was snowing and so cold. The central heating is turned off

on April 1, so we wore several jerseys under our anoraks during supper and went to bed in them …"

You could go on a trekking expedition to see these wonderful bulbs in the 'tulip belt' that extends from China westwards to Europe, including Iran, Turkey and Armenia. But it's a great deal easier to access bulbs and flowers — to buy, grow or just admire paddocks of them — in Australia.

Renowned garden designer Paul Bangay loves tulips and uses them by the thousand in his garden near Daylesford in central Victoria. "I planted about 10,000 tulips in the area with the box hedges about nine years ago," he says. "We aim for succession planting; as the late perennials are cut down, we try to get the tulips coming through. That's why we like to leave the bulbs in the ground. The trick is to plant them deeply, then they will survive."

On the other hand, many gardeners prefer to treat them as annuals. Clive Blazey, founder of The Diggers Club, says that while tulips are impressive and hugely decorative, they are the ephemera of the flowering world, most appearing for no more than two weeks a year.

"Bulbs are best planted with companion underplanting, such as alyssum or forget-me-nots, and not alone in feature beds," Clive says. "Bulbs should be the dessert while the main course is the shrubs and perennials, which provide year-round form and structure."

Paul Bangay's Tulip Tips

• The main planting season is March–April, although tulips can be planted as late as early May.

• Tulips must be planted deep in the ground. More bulbs will then survive from year to year.

• They must have a period of chill. If you live where the soil temperature in winter falls below 14 degrees, bulbs may naturalise and repeat flower. Otherwise, they are best planted as annuals.

• Tulips do not like acid soil, so be prepared to add a ration of lime if needed.

• Bulbs thrive in rich, well-drained soil. Beds or pots should be prepared with a mixed fertiliser and compost.

• Tulips are an excellent choice for containers. Be sure to use a potting mix formulated especially for bulbs.

• When the flower buds appear, use measured doses of liquid fertiliser to promote large blooms and long, strong stems so the flowers stand tall.

FACING PAGE A high brick wall provides shelter to less hardy plants and helps retain the sun's heat.

CREATING A MICROCLIMATE

*Extreme conditions such as **strong winds** or frost can make it difficult to grow plants well. The trick is to create microclimates in your garden that **provide the conditions** the plants need. Walls and fences can **shelter plants** from wind, and their sunny side will provide a **warm area** to grow frost-tender plants, particularly **fruiting trees** such as citrus.*

CHICKENS IN THE GARDEN

*Chickens **allowed to peck** and scratch in a garden keep grasses and **weeds down**. Chickens also add manure to the soil. With a fence to **keep predators**, such as foxes, at bay, the brood can be left to **roam free**. Chickens start **laying** at about five months, producing **three to four** eggs a week. They live for seven to 10 years, but are **most productive** during the first three.*

BED OF ROSES

ROSES BRING OUT GARDENING PASSIONS, AND IT'S
HARD TO AGREE ON A FAVOURITE WHEN THEY PERFORM
SO DIFFERENTLY DEPENDING ON THE CLIMATE.

'Jude the Obscure' is a David Austin rose. FACING PAGE The ever-popular 'Iceberg' is offset by precise topiary.

The massed roses include
'Grand Siècle', a hybrid
tea rose. FACING PAGE
'England's Rose', one of the
latest varieties from David
Austin, is hardy and prolific.

Roses differ greatly from place to place and from year to year. Height, colour, size and resistance to disease are all directly affected by growing conditions. Flowering times and hardiness also vary, according to the climate. Nevertheless, almost all roses will grow well enough in a wide variety of soils and climates. We all know of deserted gardens where roses have survived on benign neglect.

However, it is also true that some roses will do better than others in particular climates and that they do respond to watering. In hot dry summers, such as most Australian gardeners endure, watering prevents summer dormancy so that the plants continue to flower.

Lulled by wonderful pictures in European garden books, we need to be mindful which roses will grow well in our climate, one that is much hotter and often much drier than English or European writers comprehend.

'Climbing Peace' grows wonderfully in Australia and South Africa but is a bad performer in Ireland and a worse bloomer in Denmark. And while David Austin's superb yellow 'Graham Thomas' can reach heights of four or five metres in our gardens, in the UK it only reaches two metres.

The comparisons between different roses are endless. For example, the climbing rose 'Albertine' is seen as hardy in England, but will not survive a winter in Chicago or Prague. Here we regard it as very vigorous — great for sprawling over sheds and fences or as a windbreak.

The problem of which rose to grow is quite complicated. Twenty years ago, rose expert Susan Irvine noted: "It would be impossible to write accurately about growing roses 'in Australian conditions' because the conditions vary so radically." She found that in some of our harsher climate zones, such as Western Australia and far western Queensland, roses described as 'delicate' in English books turned out to be surprisingly robust. Susan also pointed out that in many parts of Australia it is tea roses that are the most reliable.

Barbara Wickes, who lives at Buderim in south-east Queensland, would agree: "The tea roses all do well in our area." Tea roses in Barbara's garden include 'Monsieur Tillier', 'Duchesse de Brabant' and 'Jean Ducher', while her choice of noisettes includes the beautiful 'Mme Alfred Carrière' and 'Lamarque', and other favourites such as 'Bloomfield Abundance', 'The Fairy' and 'Carefree Wonder'.

The tea roses are similar to china roses and are drought-tolerant, hence their popularity here. They get their name from their characteristic scent of china tea leaves. Noisettes are derived from an American hybrid, 'Champney's Pink Cluster', that was grown in the early 19th century. They are hardy climbers or semi-climbers, with masses of small blooms in huge clusters and generally flower continuously in hot climates.

Further south, Mulgoa architect and historian James Broadbent says the noisettes do very well in the hot summers at the base of NSW's Blue Mountains, and cope with the dry heavy clay soil.

"My favourite is 'Lamarque'," he explains. "But I also love the constantly flowering 'Safrano'." The latter was launched in France in 1839 and is regarded as one of the earliest European-bred tea roses.

"'Macartney Rose' also does well here," James says. "It makes an excellent hedging plant, although you do have to keep trimming it." A notable hybrid is 'Mermaid', bred in the UK by William Paul in 1918; its fabulous yellow flowers are not easily forgotten, and it blooms nonstop for a long time.

Gardeners in the southern states, especially Tasmania, seem to be divided equally between an ongoing love affair with David Austin's English roses and a new passion for the French varieties of George Delbard. From his first major success in 1961, 'Constance Spry' (named after the renowned English flower arranger), to his latest releases, such as 'Maid Marion' and 'The Lark Ascending', Austin has captured the imagination of gardeners everywhere with his perfumed blooms and evocative names. The Delbard roses, which often salute French painters from Matisse to Monet, are hardier in dry country gardens, according to some gardeners.

But we almost left out the ubiquitous 'Iceberg', the most widely grown rose in Australia. Bred by the German Kordes family, it came on to the market as a floribunda type in 1958 and, according to the late UK expert Peter Beales, "is surely the best of its type ever introduced".

SHAPING TOPIARY

*Topiary is the practice of **clipping** plants into **ornamental** shapes and can create a striking effect. Traditionally topiary is **shaped by the eye** but a **wire frame** can also be used. Scott Wilson made a **template** of an elephant, put it against an existing hedge and trimmed it **into shape**.*

ANNUAL REWARDS

THEIR SHOWY COLOUR HAS LONG BEEN USED AS
A GARDEN CENTREPIECE, BUT MASSED ANNUALS CAN
ALSO PROVE A TEXTURAL AND ELEGANT ADDITION.

Self-seeding Flanders poppies, giving a splash of colour. FACING PAGE *Papaver rhoeas* up close.

CLOCKWISE, FROM TOP LEFT Poppies' large brilliant blooms can be a showstopper; sweet peas will reach for the sky with a little support; poppies and *Cerinthe major* 'Purpurascens' make a striking combination; Queen Anne's lace has delicate white flowers and is easy to grow. FACING PAGE A bed filled with annuals and perennials of different colours and heights creates a rich tapestry.

FACING PAGE Keep
your annuals in flower
by removing spent
blooms regularly.

Queen Elizabeth's coronation in 1953 is regarded as a high point in the story of massed bedding of annuals. Today you might wonder why. At that time, parks and gardens in the Commonwealth were awash with beds planted in patriotic combinations of red, white and blue — stripes, Union Jacks and all manner of fancy designs. Red 'bonfire' salvia, blue lobelia and white alyssum were the favourites. And when the celebrations were over, the annuals were discarded and a whole new combination of plants emerged.

Massed beds became popular from the 1840s in Victorian England, and Australia followed this practice from the 1860s, particularly in our parks and botanical gardens. Garish colour mixtures of flowers and leaves were the norm. High maintenance and labour costs have contributed to the decline of massed bedding, and today the floral clock is the main remnant of this fashion — examples still exist in the Queen Victoria Gardens opposite Arts Centre Melbourne on St Kilda Road, and in Ballarat's Botanical Gardens. In 2015 the Royal Botanic Gardens in Sydney launched a dozen beds at Farm Cove planted in the colours of ANZAC regiments.

In nature, annuals are found mainly in open spaces where harsh environmental conditions, such as heat or extreme cold, dictate that these plants grow, bloom and set seed all within a short season. Many specimens from the wild have been 'improved' by breeders, but the best results still come from adhering to a plant's natural cycle.

Take two examples — nasturtiums and sweet peas. You may not think of these charming plants as annuals but that's what they really are. With sweet peas, deadheading is the one imperative for continual flowering. It's an agreeable task with morning coffee or an evening glass of wine. The poor plants are so desperate to set seed, they just continue to produce flowers! (To be really nice to them after a light pruning, dispense a dose of liquid fertiliser.) This is true of annuals generally … tidying up spent blooms brings rewards.

Annuals give gardeners great flexibility. They're great for filling gaps or holes in spring and late summer, and especially useful where a spring-flowering plant has finished its show and been cut back. For example, cleomes, those tall stems of 'spider' flowers, often reach nearly two metres and are great at the back of a bed.

They're a welcome addition to push through rose bushes, tired after their major flowering burst. Old-fashioned favourites, such as cosmos and snapdragons, make outstanding cut flowers. Low-growing annuals include jazzy-coloured marigolds as sun lovers and impatiens for shady sites. Both bloom for months on end.

Annuals have had a bad press in recent years with some gardeners dismissive of their many useful qualities. True, some are large and over bright, but in late summer they can look cool and elegant.

Here's a present-day suggestion for a quirky annual bed if you're feeling particularly patriotic. Try the delphinium 'Blue Butterfly'; it stands up without support to highlight the intense, dark blue single flowers. For red blooms, you could choose any number of red roses — 'Christian Dior' or any David Austin rose as a backup — or you could add to the mix the brightest salvia or zinnia you can find. For the final touch, white cosmos would be a great choice. The total effect will be more fun than a plastic flag, and more environmentally friendly, too!

Getting the Right Mix

HOW TO GROW ANNUALS WITH ROSES

It's important to avoid mixing annuals of too strong a colour with roses, as they may overwhelm the roses' usually softer colours, says David Austin, the renowned English rose breeder. He says that as well as a flower's colour, one should think about its form as a contrast. As a helpful hint about what annuals to grow with roses, he divides them into three groups that he calls 'spikes', 'plates' and 'fluffs'.

• Spikes and spires include larkspurs with their tall spires of double flowers in pastel shades; the elegantly vertical hollyhock, which suits a hot dry spot; or night-scented tobacco, *Nicotiana sylvestris*, particularly beautiful on a summer night.

• Plates — think of zinnias and sunflowers, which both thrive in summer heat. And poppies of all kinds, including the Californian variety, are good — the single flowers in pink, white and carmine, even bright yellow, are indispensable in the summer garden.

• Fluffs could include Queen Anne's lace, with wide heads of white, lacy flowers; cleome, perfect for the back of the bed with its spider-like flowers of white or pink; or old favourites such as alyssum, nigella and forget-me-not.

PATTERNS IN HEDGING
*Use a **string line** and builder's chalk to mark out a **pattern** on bare ground. For a **curved** pattern, use a piece of hose to form the first section. Mark with chalk, then **move the hose** to the next position, allowing room for the **growing plants**. Repeat until done.*

FACING PAGE Building
a rockery garden is one of
the most effective ways
to manage steep slopes.

ROCKERY GARDEN

Hillside gardening can be tricky, especially when it comes to erosion. A rockery is an **attractive**, achievable solution. A rockery **looks best** when planted with a combination of **spreading groundcovers**, mounding and bushy plants and some **upright plants** to add texture and interest. If your soil isn't **naturally rocky**, consider adding a few beautiful pieces of **local stone**.

planting guide

A GUIDE TO THE BEST PLANTS FOR EACH
SEASON — WHERE AND WHEN TO PLANT,
AND WHAT HARVEST TO EXPECT.

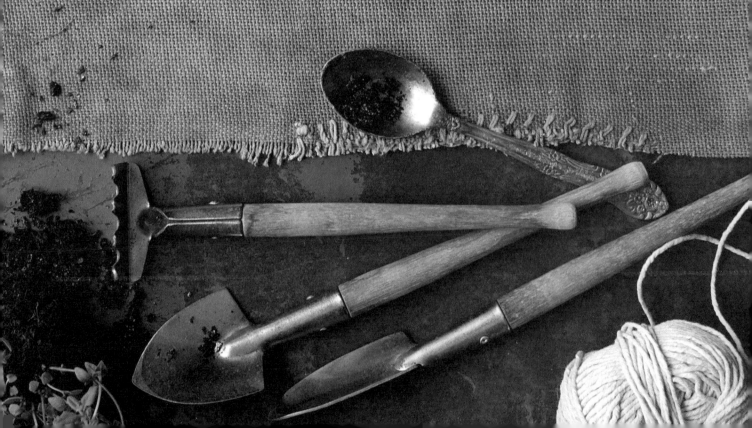

summer

December brings summer to the garden with rapid growth and shady trees.

NAME OF PLANT	HEIGHT OF PLANT	SUN OR SHADE	PLANTING ZONE
AGAPANTHUS (*Agapanthus praecox*) These old favourites are now available in many colours and forms, from dark midnight blue to mauve and pink. Select sterile hybrids to avoid weed problems.	60cm–1.8m An evergreen strappy perennial. Plant now or divide clumps in late winter.	Shade reduces flowering. Deadhead in late summer.	C M T S Tr
CEYLON SPINACH (*Basella alba*) Grow this perennial climber and you won't go short of edible greens. Attractive, with heart-shaped leaves and reddish stems. Fast-growing from seed or cutting.	3–6m Easy to control and decorative over a fence, trellis or arch.	Well-drained soil with added organic matter.	M T S Tr
DELPHINIUM (*Delphinium elatum* hybrid cultivars) Expect tall blue spires of single or double flowers. An annual in warmer climes but perennial in cool gardens.	1.2m–2m Needs staking and protection from wind.	Apply small amounts of fertiliser every two to three weeks, and water well.	C M T
ROSELLA (*Hibiscus sabdariffa*) Harvest the edible flowers as the calyces swell to make jams, syrup, preserves (delicious in sparkling wine) and as the basis for hibiscus tea.	2m Spindly shrub with yellow flowers that needs a long growing season.	Cover with fine gauze to protect plants from beetle pests. Water well.	M T S Tr

Enjoy gardening in January during the cool of the morning or evening.

NAME OF PLANT	HEIGHT OF PLANT	SUN OR SHADE	PLANTING ZONE
ALYSSUM (*Lobularia maritima*) Forms a carpet of tiny white, mauve or deep rose flowers. Grows readily from scattered seed. Use it to fill gaps in the garden, edge a pot or to grow between paving stones.	10cm–25cm Annual groundcover that's attractive to bees and other pollinating insects.	Needs little care. Remove when plants get spindly and plant fresh.	C M T S

KEY   Sun   Semi-Shade   Shade

C = Cool climate   M = Mediterranean   T = Temperate   S = Subtropical   Tr = Tropical

NAME OF PLANT	HEIGHT OF PLANT	SUN OR SHADE	PLANTING ZONE
CHERRY TOMATO (*Solanum lycopersicum* syn. *Lycopersicon esculentum*) Superbly easy to grow and even resists fruit fly. Plant seedlings now for late summer lunch boxes and salads.	1–2.5m Plants sprawl, so staking or trellising makes them easier to manage and harvest.	Water regularly. Fertilise weekly once flowering starts.	C M T S Tr
EVOLVULUS (*Evolvulus glomeratus* 'Blue My Mind') Evolvulus is a dwarf, blue-flowered shrub for gardens, pots or hanging baskets. Thrives in the heat and tolerates mild frost.	40cm Spreads by rhizomes to form a dense, mounding groundcover, 50cm across.	Water when summers are dry, but keep foliage dry in winter.	M T S Tr
RED FLOWERING GUM (*Corymbia ficifolia* 'Summer Red') Large red flowers smother these compact trees in mid to late summer. There are also pink, orange and white varieties.	4–5m Evergreen tree with a rounded head — ideal for small gardens.	Protect from frost while trees are small. Prune after flowering.	C M T S Tr
WALLFLOWER (*Erysimum cheiri*) Sow seeds or plant seedlings now and into autumn. The heads of yellow, orange or brown-toned flowers look good in the garden or picked for a posy.	40–60cm Select compact varieties for containers or small beds.	Sow seeds in punnets and transplant into prepared garden beds.	C M T S Tr

It's the height of summer, but if you're keen to plant there are still a few options in February.

NAME OF PLANT	HEIGHT OF PLANT	SUN OR SHADE	PLANTING ZONE
HIBISCUS (*Alyogyne huegelii*) Fast-growing, with a succession of single, blue to mauve flowers over summer. Suitable for pots, native gardens or mass-planted in a shrubbery.	2m Keep compact by pruning after each flower flush or in late summer.	Plant now. Apply low-phosphorus fertiliser in spring.	C M T S Tr
NAKED LADY (*Amaryllis belladonna*) The buds open into large pink or white trumpet flowers in late summer and autumn. While dormant, these plants survive fire and summer drought.	30cm Plant the large bulbs in summer, or look for flowering plants in containers.	Tolerates a spot that's dry in summer. Don't bury bulbs; neck should be exposed.	C M T S
POMEGRANATE (*Punica granatum*) The orange flowers are followed by large, red fruit. Inside the woody skin are juicy seeds. Ideal for that dry northerly or westerly situation where little else grows.	3–5m A dense, deciduous shrub or small tree. Dwarf flowering forms suit containers.	Survives heat, frost, drought and neglect but needs good drainage.	C M T S Tr
SALVIA 'HOT LIPS' (*Salvia microphylla* 'Hot Lips') Among the many varieties, 'Hot Lips' can add a wow factor to summer gardens. White flowers are tipped with bright red 'lips'.	90cm A quick and easy perennial; grow from cutting in late summer or buy in flower.	Shelter in cold winters; prune after flowering.	C M T S Tr

autumn

Remove spent summer crops in March to make way for these cool-season beauties.

NAME OF PLANT	HEIGHT OF PLANT	SUN OR SHADE	PLANTING ZONE
CAULIFLOWER (*Brassica oleracea* var. *botrytis*) An annual crop that's part of the Brassicaceae family — these vegetables have proven cancer-fighting properties.	**30cm+** The edible 'curd' emerges from a circle of large, attractive, green-blue leaves.	Cauliflowers are quite decorative — colours include white, lime, orange and purple.	C M T S Tr
CHIVES (*Allium schoenoprasum*) A perennial herb with pretty pink edible flowers, but grown for its fine, tubular leaves. Harvest by snipping the leaves at the base.	**20–50cm** Chives grow in little upright clumps. Now's the time to divide them if the clumps are too thick.	Any bright spot can fit a pot of chives. Good companion plants for carrot, lettuce and cucumber.	C M T S Tr
CORNFLOWER (*Centaurea cyanus*) This is the common cornflower, a tough annual and a good cut or dried flower. Its many other names include 'bachelor's buttons' and 'break-your-spectacles'.	**60cm–1m** Upright annual with silver-grey foliage and blue, pink or white thistle-like flowers.	Excellent in the cottage garden. Choose a spot sheltered from wind, with good drainage.	C M T S
FREESIA (*Freesia alba*) Hailing from a Mediterranean-style climate in South Africa, these perennials are often grown as annuals. They bring colour and perfume to the early spring garden.	**10–15cm** Beyond the common whites are hybrids with longer stems, double blooms and vibrant colours.	For spring flowers, plant the bulbs now in pots or beds or to naturalise under trees.	C M T S
LEEK (*Allium ampeloprasum* var. *porrum*) Technically a biennial, but grown as an annual, leeks offer a milder flavour than onions and are easy to grow from seed. A versatile kitchen staple.	**60cm–1.5m** Upright, sometimes very tall, with fan-shaped leaves.	Space seedlings 15–20cm apart. Leeks take six months to mature.	C T S
LETTUCE (*Lactuca sativa*) A fast-cropping leafy green that's actually a member of the daisy family. There are two main types of lettuce: hearting, and loose leaf or 'cut and come again'.	**30cm** The cooler months favour the hearting types, such as cos. Give them room to bulk up.	This speedy crop is ideal to plant between slower-growing vegetables. Good in pots, too.	C M T S Tr

KEY   Sun   Semi-Shade   Shade

C = Cool climate   M = Mediterranean   T = Temperate   S = Subtropical   Tr = Tropical

April is a smart time to do some long-term planning in the garden.

NAME OF PLANT	HEIGHT OF PLANT	SUN OR SHADE	PLANTING ZONE
BROAD BEAN (*Vicia faba*) These weak-stemmed plants need the support of string and stakes around the bed, or should be trained against a trellis.	1–2m Tall forms can grow up to two metres; dwarf forms around one.	Shelter from strong winds. Cold weather delays beans forming.	C M T S Tr
DAFFODIL (*Narcissus* spp. and hybrids) Popular late winter to spring bulb. Jonquils and paperwhite narcissus are some of the best choices for warmer areas.	50–60cm For pots or small spaces, grow miniatures, such as 'Tete-a-Tete', to 25cm tall.	Plant 10–15cm deep. Deadhead and feed for next year's blooms.	C M T S
LEMON (*Citrus limon*) Productive small tree. Remove lemons in the first year, as the branches may be too weak to support their weight.	1.5–8m Dwarf varieties suit large pots. 'Eureka' and 'Meyer' crop over a long period.	Plant in a warm spot protected from frost and wind in well-drained soil.	C M T S Tr

May is the time to plant roses, winter vegetables and spring bulbs.

NAME OF PLANT	HEIGHT OF PLANT	SUN OR SHADE	PLANTING ZONE
CHRYSANTHEMUM (*Chrysanthemum* x *grandiflorum*) Potted plants in flower are available to celebrate Mother's Day.	50cm–1m Tall garden varieties need staking.	Cut back potted gifts after flowers finish and plant out.	C M T S
FLANDERS POPPY (*Papaver rhoeas*) This red-flowering annual is the symbol of Remembrance Day (November 11) and blooms in late spring. Scatter seeds where they are to grow.	60cm Mass plant or add patches among other plants for spring colour.	Thin seedlings until about 30cm apart.	C M T S
KALE (*Brassica oleracea*) A tall-growing, leafy winter vegetable that can be harvested a few leaves at a time, as required.	60cm Liquid feed every two weeks for optimum growth.	Sometimes referred to as a super food, kale is packed with nutrients.	C M T S Tr
ROSE (*Rosa* hybrids) Plant bare-rooted roses — available now and through winter — in soil improved with added manure and compost.	30cm–5m Roses range from ground covers and miniatures to shrubs and climbers.	Full sun is a must for strong, healthy growth.	C M T S

winter

Winter is here — June is the time to plant bare-rooted trees and enjoy potted colour.

NAME OF PLANT	HEIGHT OF PLANT	SUN OR SHADE	PLANTING ZONE
FLAMING KATY (*Kalanchoe blossfeldiana*) Long-flowering succulent for winter colour in pots indoors, on balconies or in gardens.	20–40cm Red, orange, yellow, pink or white flowers with attractive scalloped leaves.	☀ Allow potted plants to dry out between watering. Remove spent blooms.	C M T S
GLOBE ARTICHOKE (*Cynara scolymus*) Take suckers from mature clumps. Plant 1m apart in well-drained soil. Fertilise after planting.	1m Striking leafy clumps in an ornamental garden, orchard or vegetable patch.	☀ Harvest edible flower buds in spring. Unharvested buds open to purple thistle flowers.	C M T S
JAPANESE MAPLE (*Acer palmatum*) Select trees for their autumn leaf shade. Some varieties also have colourful new leaves in spring.	1.5m–7m Grafted weeping forms suit courtyard gardens or large containers.	☀ ☁ Protect from hot summer sun.	C M T
POLYANTHUS (*Primula* x *polyantha*) Grown as a brightly flowered annual for winter colour in pots or gardens. Plant seedlings or advanced plants.	15–20cm Ideal for containers but keep them well watered, especially in windy conditions.	☀ ☁ Deadhead to keep plants blooming through winter and spring.	C M T S

July may be rug-up weather, but there's still lots to plant in the garden as you plan ahead.

NAME OF PLANT	HEIGHT OF PLANT	SUN OR SHADE	PLANTING ZONE
ASPARAGUS (*Asparagus officinalis*) Plant crowns (dormant roots) in winter at least 1m apart, in their own bed for ease of care and harvesting.	1m Spears quickly expand into tall feathery fronds if left unharvested.	☀ To allow plants to become established, wait for the third year to harvest.	C M T S

KEY   ☀ Sun   ☁ Semi-Shade   ☁ Shade

C = Cool climate   M = Mediterranean   T = Temperate   S = Subtropical   Tr = Tropical

DWARF CLEOME (*Cleome* 'Señorita Rosalita') Compact and almost thornless, this variety will provide months of mauve flowers that are sterile but attract beneficial insects.	30–60cm Ideal for containers or grow as an easy and colourful garden plant.	Good drought and heat tolerance. Low maintenance.	C M T S Tr
HELLEBORE (*Helleborus orientalis*) These long-lasting, delicate blooms light up a winter garden. Choose white, pink, green or slate-toned flowers.	40cm An attractive, leafy perennial to grow under trees or in a pot.	Provide summer shade and regular water in warmer areas.	C M T
NSW WARATAH (*Telopea speciosissima*) This evergreen native shrub blooms from late winter to spring with showy heads of red. Long-lasting cut flower.	2–4m Tall shrub. Keep compact by light pruning after flowering.	Well-drained acidic soil is a must, as is low phosphorus fertiliser.	C M T S
SEEDLESS VALENCIA ORANGE (*Citrus* x *aurantium*, syn. *C.* x *sinensis*) Crops from mid-winter. Fruit has few seeds and holds on the tree for months.	3–5m Apply citrus food in late winter and late summer for healthy growth.	Good drainage vital for all citrus. Dwarf forms are ideal for pots.	M T S Tr

Early bulbs are in bloom during August and spring is on the way — time to get planting!

NAME OF PLANT	HEIGHT OF PLANT	SUN OR SHADE	PLANTING ZONE
AZALEA (*Rhododendron indica* hybrids syn. *Azalea indica*) These massed white, pink, red or purple flowers are great from late winter to spring.	50cm–3m Evergreen shrubs are top choices as container plants in shade or to grow under trees.	Acid soil or potting mix is best. Lightly prune and feed after flowering.	C M T S
CARROT (*Daucus carota* subsp. *sativus*) Carrots are available in a variety of sizes and colours. Plant seed now for harvest in late spring and enjoy orange, red, purple or white carrots.	20cm Ferny stalks produce an edible root ready to harvest around three months from sowing seed.	Deep, sandy soils and regular watering. Grow small varieties in containers or shallow soils.	C M T S Tr
GINGER (*Zingiber officinale*) Cut back stems in autumn or winter. Harvest pieces of rhizome as needed from autumn to early spring. Divide clumps in winter or spring.	1–1.5m The tall, leafy canes develop and flower through spring and summer.	Plant rhizomes in late winter or early spring in well-drained, rich soil. Protect from frost.	T S Tr
POTATO (*Solanum tuberosum*) Virus-free seed potatoes planted now in 15cm-deep furrows produce kilograms in summer. Begin digging spuds as plants bloom and die back.	30–40cm A leafy, frost-tender annual vegetable, whose bounty lies beneath the soil's surface.	Water regularly. Mound soil around plant base to keep potatoes well covered.	C M T S Tr

spring

September is not only the beginning of spring, it's also a great time to plant.

NAME OF PLANT	HEIGHT OF PLANT	SUN OR SHADE	PLANTING ZONE
CRABAPPLE (*Malus floribunda*) In bloom with a mass of pink buds and white flowers, crabapples shout that spring is here. Fruit can be harvested in late summer to make jams and jellies.	3.5–5m Rounded, many-branched tree. For a smaller tree, select a cultivar such as *Malus ioensis* 'Plena'.	Prune after flowering or in early winter, if necessary, to remove congested growth.	C M T S
MANDEVILLA (*Mandevilla sanderi* and other species) A twining climber with pink, red or white trumpet flowers from spring to autumn or early winter.	5m A lush, fast-growing climber to grow on a trellis or arch, or to twine up a pole.	May die back in cold or frosty zones where mandevillas need a warm microclimate.	C M T S Tr
TOMATO (*Solanum lycopersicum*) Myriad heirloom and modern varieties grow from spring to autumn. Cherry varieties are basically foolproof.	60cm–2.5m This frost-tender vegetable needs the support of stakes or a trellis. Patio varieties suit pots.	Water regularly (at least daily on hot or windy days). Fertilise weekly once flowering starts. Protect from fruit fly.	C M T S Tr
ZINNIA (*Zinnia elegans*) These bright and cheerful annuals are grown for summer colour or as a cut flower. Blooms are usually red, pink, orange, yellow or white.	30cm–1.5m A quick-growing annual from seed or seedling. Plant during spring.	Zinnias relish hot and dry conditions; a good choice for warm, inland areas.	C M T S Tr

October is mid-spring, so take time to smell the flowers.

NAME OF PLANT	HEIGHT OF PLANT	SUN OR SHADE	PLANTING ZONE
AFRICAN MARIGOLD (*Tagetes* hybrid cultivars) Plant seedlings now to add a punch of bold colour to the garden, pots or vegetable beds through summer.	30–50cm Sow seed or plant seedlings during spring for summer flowers.	Water regularly, liquid feed. Check leaves and backs of flowers for snails.	C M T S Tr

KEY   ☀ Sun   ☁ Semi-Shade   ☁ Shade

C = Cool climate   M = Mediterranean   T = Temperate   S = Subtropical   Tr = Tropical

NAME OF PLANT	HEIGHT OF PLANT	SUN OR SHADE	PLANTING ZONE
CAPSICUM (*Capsicum annuum*) Plant summer vegetable seedlings, including capsicum, in the garden or in large containers. Capsicums can be harvested green but become sweeter as they colour.	**50cm–1m** Shrubby perennials usually grown as annuals. Stake in windy positions.	Water regularly, liquid feed. Use organic baits to protect from fruit fly.	C M T S Tr
KANGAROO PAW (*Anigozanthos flavidus*) This native perennial has paw-shaped flowers from spring to autumn. Held above the strappy leaves, the flowers are usually green, yellow, orange or red.	**50cm–1m** Remove spent flower stems and cut back untidy growth after flowering.	Select a spot with excellent drainage. Use low-phosphorus fertiliser.	C M T S
SCARLET RUNNER BEANS (*Phaseolus coccineus*) Can be picked as green beans or allowed to dry for an autumn harvest. Best in cool climates. Sow seeds in spring.	**1.8m** Twining perennial vine also known as 'seven-year bean'.	Support on stakes or a trellis. Water well in summer.	C M
'SWEET SPOT' ROSE (*Rosa* 'Sweet Spot') Developed for containers and small spaces. A new variety with multi-toned flowers in pink, yellow and orange. Blooms appear from spring to autumn.	**80cm** Small and bushy with masses of colourful flowers.	Apply slow-release fertiliser in spring and summer; water containers daily.	C M T S Tr

November is late spring but morphing fast into summer.

NAME OF PLANT	HEIGHT OF PLANT	SUN OR SHADE	PLANTING ZONE
BROMELIAD (*Aechmea fasciata* and other species) Grow bromeliads for colourful leaves and long-lasting red flowers. Buy potted or detach offshoots from established plants.	**15cm–2m** Rosette-shaped plants are ideal for mass planting under trees. Select a frost-free spot.	Grow in well-drained, coarse potting mix or bark, or attach to logs.	C M T S Tr
EGGPLANT (*Solanum melongena*) Also known as aubergine, it's ripe for harvesting in summer and autumn. As well as the large, purple-black fruit there are white, orange and finger-sized varieties.	**60cm–1.5m** Attractive, bushy plant with violet-blue flowers that are quickly followed by fruit.	Sow seed in well-drained soil, water regularly, apply fertiliser as flowering begins.	C M T S Tr
HYDRANGEA (*Hydrangea macrophylla*) These shrubs are smothered with blousy heads of blue, purple, pink or white flowers in summer. In cold climates, flowers age to pink and green.	**1–3m** Compact, long-flowering 'Endless Summer' varieties suit containers.	Water heavily on hot days, prune after flowering or in winter. Acid soils encourage blue flowers.	C M T S
WATERMELON (*Citrullus lanatus*) Grows easily from seed sown directly into the soil. Needs a lengthy, warm season (74–85 days or more) to ripen, so does best in areas with long, hot summers.	**1.5m** These spreading annual vines can occupy 3–6 square metres of ground.	Best results from copious watering and regular fertilising as plants grow.	M T S Tr

Creating a garden is a magical art and we are very grateful to all the gardeners who have opened their gates to *Country Style* readers over the years. A very special thank you must go to our gardening contributor Christine Reid who has travelled all over Australia to write many of the stories included in this book. She is always very generous when it comes to sharing her extensive gardening knowledge with our team. The stories in this book have been collected by our dedicated writers over the years — for, just like a garden, nothing grows overnight. Art director Sharon Misko's talented eye and great ideas — as well as her calm disposition — make her a pleasure to work with. I also wanted to thank the *Country Style* team, particularly our chief subeditor Greg Taylor, who worked on this book while navigating the usual deadlines for the magazine — they all did a wonderful job. And finally a big thank you to publisher Catherine Milne for allowing us to create this book.

HarperCollins*Publishers*

First published in Australia in 2016
by HarperCollins*Publishers* Australia Pty Limited
ABN 36 009 913 517
harpercollins.com.au

HarperCollins*Publishers*
Level 13, 201 Elizabeth Street, Sydney, NSW 2000, Australia
Unit D1, 63 Apollo Drive, Rosedale, Auckland 0632, New Zealand
A 53, Sector 57, Noida, UP, India
1 London Bridge Street, London, SE1 9GF, United Kingdom
2 Bloor Street East, 20th floor, Toronto, Ontario M4W 1A8, Canada
195 Broadway, New York, NY 10007, USA

COUNTRYSTYLE

Editor-in-chief: Victoria Carey
Creative director: Giota Letsios
Melbourne editor: Virginia Imhoff
Chief subeditor: Greg Taylor
Food features editor: Sarah Neil
Art director: Jo Quarmby
Junior designer: Kristina Harrison
Editorial coordinator: Anna Delprat

Book editor: Christine Reid
Cover and design: Sharon Misko
Subediting: Greg Taylor and Catherine McCormack
Front cover photography: Sharyn Cairns
Back cover photography: Claire Tackas
Title page and end paper illustrations: Daniella Germain

Contributing writers: Judy Adamson, Karen Cotton, Jacqueline Forster, Ali Gripper,
Virginia Imhoff, Claire Mactaggart, Catherine McCormack, Carolyn Parfitt, Christine Reid,
Amy Richardson, Gretel Sneath, Jennifer Stackhouse, Megan Trousdale
Contributing photographers: Brigid Arnott, Sharyn Cairns, Jared Fowler, Simon Griffiths,
Simon Kenny, Anson Smart, Claire Takacs, Alicia Taylor, Michael Wee
Contributing stylists: Indianna Foord, Louise Marshall

National Library of Australia cataloguing-in-publication data:

Country style gardens / Country Style magazine.
ISBN: 978 0 7322 9997 2 (paperback)
Gardens — Australia.
Country homes — Australia.
Country life — Australia.
Lifestyles — Australia.
Country Style Magazine.
635.0994

Colour reproduction by Graphic Print Group, Adelaide
Printed and bound in China by R. R. Donnelley

5 4 3 2   16 17 18 19